THOMAS NASH

Lenten Stuff

1599

SCOLAR PRESS 1971

Printed in Great Britain by
The Scolar Press Limited
Menston, Yorkshire, England

NOTE

Reproduced (original size) from a copy in the Bodleian Library, by permission of the Curators. Shelf-mark: Tanner 218.

Nash explains in the opening remarks of his *Lenten Stuff* how he was obliged to leave London and seek refuge in Great Yarmouth because of the "troublesome stir" caused by his play *The Isle of Dogs*. There are no extant copies of this play, but from Nash's remarks it would seem that he was not the sole author, and that it was a performance in the summer of 1597 which started the trouble. The time he spent in Yarmouth proved to be most enjoyable and he wrote *Lenten Stuff* in praise of the town and its red herrings. The work was also undoubtedly undertaken to demonstrate Nash's expertise as a writer — to prove that he could write well, even about herrings.

Lenten Stuff was entered in the *Stationers' Register* to Cuthbert Burby on 11th January 1598/99, but the Stationers' Company still regarded anything written by Nash with suspicion, and the entry reads:

> Entred . . . in full Court holden this Daie a booke
> called the praise of the Redd herringe upon Condicon
> that he [Burby] gett yt Laufully Aucthorised.
> (E. Arber (ed.) *A Transcript of the Registers of the Company of Stationers of London*, Vol. III, 1875-77, p. 134.)

Under the circumstances publication must have taken place rapidly and, although the exact date of publication is unknown, it must have been before 1st June 1599, since on that date the Stationers' Company put a complete ban on all Nash's work and resolved:

> That all Nasshes bookes and Doctor Harvyes bookes
> be taken wheresoever they maye be found and that
> none of theire bookes bee ever printed hereafter.
> (*ibid.*, p. 677)

Lenten Stuff was reprinted in the *Harleian Miscellany*, Vol. VI, 1745, and again in Vol. II, 1809, and Vol. VI, 1810. Further editions have appeared by C. Hindley in *Miscellanea Antiqua Anglicana*, Vol. I, 1871; A. B. Grosart in *Works*, Vol. V, 1883-84; R. B. McKerrow in *Works*, Vol. III, 1905, reprinted 1958; and R. Ashley and E. M. Moseley in *Elizabethan Fiction*, 1953.

Reference: STC. 18370.

Thom. Tanner.

NASHES
Lenten Stuffe,

Containing,
The Description and first Procrea-
tion and Increase of the towne of
Great Yarmouth in
Norffolke:

With a new Play neuer played before, of the
praise of the RED
HERRING.

Fitte of all Clearkes of Noblemens Kitchins to be
read: and not vnnecessary by all Seruing men
that haue short boord-wages, to be remembred.

Famam peto per vndas.

LONDON
Printed for N. L. and C. B. and are to be
sold at the west end of Paules.
1599.

a

To his worthie good patron, Lu-
ſtie Humfrey, according as the townſ-
men doo chriſten him, little Numps as the
Nobilitie and Courtiers do name him, and Honeſt
Humſrey, as all his friendes and acquaintance eſteeme
him, King of the Tobacconiſts *hic & vbique,* and a ſingu-
lar Mecœnas to the Pipe and the Tabour (as his patient
liuery attendant can witneſſe) his bounden Orator
T. N. moſt proſtrately offers vp this tribute
of inke and paper.

Oſt courteous vnlearned lo-
uer of Poetry, and yet a Po-
et thy ſelfe, of no leſſe price
then H. S. that in honour of
Maid-marrian giues ſweete
Margerã for his Empreſſe,
and puttes the Sowe moſt
ſawcily vppon ſome great
perſonage, what euer ſhe bee,
bidding her (as it runnes in
the old ſong) Go from my
Garden go, for there no flowers for thee dooth grow.
Theſe be to notifie to your diminutiue excelſitude, and compendi-
ate greatneſſe, what my zeale is towardes you, that in no ſtreigh-
ter bonds woulde bee pounded and enliſted, then in an Epiſtle
Dedicatorie. Too many more luſty-bloud Brauamente ſegniors,
with Cales *beards, as broade as ſcullers maples, that they make*

A 2   *cleane*

The Epiftle

cleane their boates with, could I haue turned it ouer, and had nothing for my labour, fome faire woords except, of, goodfir will it
pleafe you to come neere, and drinke a cuppe of wine? after my returne from Ireland I doubt not but my fortunes will be of fome
growth to requite you   In the meane time my fword is at your
commaund, and before God, money fo fcatteringly runnes heere
and there vppon vtenfilia furnitures, ancients, and other neceffary preparations, (and which is a double charge, looke how much
Tobacco wee carry with vs to expell cold, the like quantitie of
Staues-aker wee muft prouide vs of to kill lice in that rugged
countrey of rebels) that I fay vnto you in the word of a martia-
lift, wee cannot doo as wee would. I am no incredulous Didimus,
but haue more fayth to beleeue they haue no coyne, then they
haue meanes to fupplie themfelues with it, and fo leaue them. To
any other carpetmunger or primerofe knight of Primero, bring I
a dedication and the dice ouer night haue not befriended him, hee
fleepes fiue dayes and fiue nights to new skin his beautie, and will
not bee knowne hee is awakt till his men vppon their owne bondes
(a difmall world for trenchermen, when theyr maifters bond fhal
not be fo good as theirs) haue tooke vp commodities or frefh droppings of the minte for him : and then, what then? he payes for the
ten dozen of balles hee left vppon the fcore at the tennis court,
hee fendes for his Barber to depure, decuriate, and fpunge him,
whome hauing not paide a twelmonth before, he now raines downe
eight quarter angels into his hande, to make his liberalitie feeme
greater, and giues him a caft riding ierkin, and an olde Spanifh
hatte into the bargaine, and Gods peace bee with him. The chamber is not ridde of the fmell of his feet, but the greafie fhoomaker
with his fquirrels skin, and a whole ftall of ware vppon his arme
enters, and wrencheth his legges for an houre togither, and after
fhewes his tally. By S. Loy that drawes deepe, and by that time
his Tobacco marchant is made euen with, and hee hath dinde at
a tauerne, and flept his vnder-meale at a bawdy houfe, his purfe
is on the heild, and only fortie fhillings hee hath behinde, to trie
his fortune with at the cardes in the prefence, which if it profper,
                                                              the

Dedicatorie.

the court cannot containe him, but to London againe he will, to renell it ,and haue two playes in one night, invite all the Poets and Musitions to his chamber the next morning, where against theyr comming, a whole heape of money shall bee bespread uppon the boord ,and all his trunkes opened to shewe his rich sutes, but the deuill a whit hee bestowes on them , saue bottle ale and Tobacco: and desires a generall meeting.

The particular of it is that bounty is bankerupt, and Lady sensualitie licks all the fat fro the seuen Liberal Sciences, that Poetry, if it were not a trick to please, my Lady would bee excluded out of Christian buriall, and in steade of wreathes of lawrell to crowne it with haue a bell with a cocks combe clapt on the crowne of it by olde Iohannes de Indagines , and his quire of dorbellists. Wherefore the premisses considered (I pray you consider of that woord Premisses, for somewhere I haue borrowed it) neither to rich ,noble, right worshipfull, or worshipfull, of spirituall or temporall, will I consecrate this woorke, but to thee and thy capering humour alone, that if thy starres had doone thee right, they should haue made thee one of the mightiest princes of Germany, not for thou canst driue a coach ,or kill an oxe so wel as they ,but that thou art neuer wel ,but when thou art amongst the retinue of the Muses, and there spendest more in the twinckling of an eye , then in a whole yeare thou gettest by some grasierly gentilitie thou followest. A King thou art by name, and a King of good fellowshippe by nature, whereby I ominate this Encomion of the king of fishes was predestinate to thee from thy swadling clothes. Hugge it , mole it , kisse it , and cull it now thou hast it, & renounce eating of greene beefe and garlike, till Martlemas, if it be not the next stile to The Strife of Loue in a Dreame, or, the Lamentable burning of Teuerton. Giue mee good words I beseech thee, though thou giuest me nothing else, and thy words shal stand for thy deeds, which I will take as well in woorth, as if they were the deedes and euidences of all the lande thou hast. Heere I bring you a redde herring, if you will finde drinke to it , there an ende , no other detriments will I putte you to. Let the Kanne of strong ale your

A 3   constable,

The Epiſtle Dedicatorie.

conſtable, with the toaſte his browne bilh, and ſugar and nutmegs
his watchmen ſtande in a readineſſe , to entertaine mee euerie
time I come by your lodging. In Ruſcia there are no preſents but
of meate or drinke; I preſent you with meate, and you in honou-
rable courteſie to requite mee , can do no leſſe then preſent mee
with the beſt mornings draught of merry-go-downe in your quar-
ters, and ſo I kiſſe the ſhadow of your feetes ſhadow , amiable
Donſell, expecting your ſacred Poeme of the Hermites
Tale, that will reſtore the golden age amongſt
vs, and ſo vppon my ſoules knees,
I take myleaue.

Yours for a whole laſt of redde
Herrings.

Th. Naſhe.

To his Readers, hee cares not what they be.

Afhes *Lentenftuffe* : and why *Nafhes Lentenftuffe?* fome fcab-bed fcald fquire replies, becaufe I had money lent me at *Yar-mouth,*and I pay them againe in prayfe of their towne and the redde herring, and if it were fo goodman Pig-wiggen,were not that honeft dealing, pay thou al thy debtes fo if thou canft for thy life,but thou art a Ninnihammer: that is not it, therefore *Nickneacaue* I cal it *Nafhes Lenten-ftuffe,*as well for it was moft of my ftudy the laft Lent,as that we vfe fo to term any fifh that takes falt, of which the Red Herring is one the apteft. O but fayth another *Iphn Dringle*, there is a booke of the *Red Herrings taile* printed foure Termes fince, that made this ftale. Let it be a taile of habberdine if it will,I am nothing entaild thereunto,I fcorne it, I fcorne it,that my woorkes fhould turne taileto any man. Head, body, taileand all of a redde Her-ring you fhall haue of mee, if that will pleafe you, or if that will not pleafe you, ftay till Efter Terme, and then with the anfwere to the *Trim Tram*, I will make you laugh your hearts out. Take me at my woord,for I am the man that will doo it. This is a light friskin of my witte, like the prayfe of iniuftice, the feuer quartaine, *Bufiris* or *Phalaris,*wherin I fol-low the trace of the famoufeft fchollers of all ages, whom

To the Reader.

whom a wantonizing humour once in their life time hath possest to play with strawes, and turne mole-hils into mountaines.

Euery man can say,Bee to a Battledore, and write in prayse of Vertue,and the seuen Liberall Sciences, thresh corne out of the full sheaues, and fetch water out of the Thames; but out of drie stubble to make an after haruest , and a plentifull croppe without sowing,and wring iuice out of a flint, thats *Pierce a Gods name,* and the right tricke of a workman. Let me speake to you about my huge woords which I vse in this booke, and then you are your own men to do what you list. Know it is my true vaine to be *tragicus Orator,*and of all stiles I most affect & striue to imitate *Aretines,* not caring for this demure soft *mediocre genus*;that is, like water and wine mixt togither,but giue me pure wine of it self, & that begets good bloud, and heates the brain thorowly: I had as lieue haue no sunne,as haue it shine faintly, no fire, as a smothering fire of small coales, no cloathes, rather then weare linsey wolsey. Apply it for me, for I am cald away to correct the faults of the presse,that escaped in my absence from the Prin-ting-house.

THE PRAISE OF
the red herring.

He ſtraunge turning of the Ile of
Dogs, frõ a commedie to a tragedie
two ſummers paſt, with the trou-
bleſome ſtir which hapned aboute
it, is a generall rumour that hath fil-
led all England, and ſuch a heauie
croſſe laide vpon me , as had well
neere confounded mee : I meane,
not ſo much in that it ſequeſtred
me from the woonted meanes of my maintenance, which is
as great a maime to any mans happineſſe, as can bee feared
from the hands of miſerie, or the deepe pit of diſpaire wher-
into I was falne, beyond my greateſt friendes reach to recouer mee : but that in my exile and irkeſome diſcontented a-
bandonment, the ſillieſt millers thombe , or contemptible
ſtickle-banck of my enemies, is as buſie nibbling about my
fame, as if I were a deade man throwne amongeſt them to
feede vpon. So I am I confeſſe in the worldes outwarde
apparance , though perhappes I may prooue a cunninger
diuer then they are aware , which if it ſo happen as I am
partely aſſured , and that I plunge aboue water once a-
gaine , let them looke to it , for I will put them in bryne ,
or a piteous pickle euery one. But let that paſſe, though
they ſhal find I wil not let it paſſe when time ſerues, I hauing a pamphlet hot a brooding that ſhall be called the

Quaſſa tamen
noſtra eſt, non
merſa nec ob-
rutunauis.

B. *Bar-*

Barbers warming panne, and to the occasion, afresh of my falling in alliance with this lenten argument. That infortunate imperfit Embrion of my idle houres the Ile of Dogs before mentioned, breeding vnto me such bitter throwes in the teaming as it did, and the tempestes that arose at his birth, so astonishing outragious and violent as if my braine had bene conceiued of another Hercules, I was so terrifyed with my owne encrease (like a woman long trauailing to bee deliuered of a monster) that it was no sooner borne but I was glad to run from it. Too inconsiderate headlong rashnesse this may be censured in me, in beeing thus prodigall in aduantaging my aduersaries, but my case is no smoothred secret, and with light cost of rough cast rethoricke it may be tollerably playstered ouer, if vnder the pardon and priuiledge of incensed higher powers it were lawfully indulgenst me freely to aduocate my owne astrology. Sufficeth what they in their graue wisedoomes shall proscribe, I in no sorte will seeke to acquite, nor presumptuously attempte to dispute against the equity of their iudgementes, but humble and prostrate appeale to their mercies. Auoide or giue grounde I did, *scriptum est* I will not goe from it, and *post varios casus*, variable Knight arrant aduentures, and outroades, and inroades, at greate Yarmouth in Norfolke, I ariued in the latter ende of Autumne. Where hauing scarse lookt about me, my presaging minde saide to it selfe, *Hic fanonius serenus est, hic auster imbricus*, this is a predestinate fit place for *Pierse Pennilesse* to set vp his staffe in. Therein not much diameter to my deuining hopes did the euent sort it selfe, for sixe weekes first and last vnder that predodumant constellation of *Aquariis* or *Ioues Nectar* filler, tooke I vp my repose, and there mette with such kind entertainment and benigne hospitality when I was *Vna litera plusquam* * *medicus* as Plautus saith, and not able to line to my selfe with my owne iuice, as some of the crummes of it like the crums in a bushy beard after a greate banquet, will remaine in my papers to bee seene when I am

dead

* An imperfit Embrio I ma well call it, for I hauing begun out the induction and first act of it, the other foure acts without my consent, or the east guesse of my drift or scope, by the players were supplied, which pred both their trouble and mine to.

Medicus.

deade and vnder ground; from the bare perufing of which
infinite pofterities of hungry Poets fhall receiue good refre-
fhing, euen as *Homer* by *Galatæon* was pictured vomiting in
a bafó (in the temple that *Ptolomy Philopater* erected to him)
and the reft of the fucceeding Poets after him, greedily lap-
ping vp what he difgorged. That good old blind bibber of
Helicon I wot well, came a begging to one of the chiefe citties of Greece,& promifed them vaft corpulent volumes of
immortallity, if they would beftowe vpon him but a flender
outbrothers annuity of muttó & broth, and a pallet to fleep
on, and with derifion they reiected him, wherupon he went
to their enemies with the like proffer, who vfed him honourably, and whome hee vfed fo honourably, that to this daye
though it be three thoufand yeare fince, their name and glo-
rie florifh greene in mens memory through his induftry. I
trufte you make no queftion but thofe dull pated pennifa-
thers, that in fuch dudgen fcorne reiected him, drunck deep
of the foure cup of repentance for it, when the high flight of
his lines in common brute was ooyeffed. Yea in the worde
of one no more wealthy then hee was, wealthy faide I, nay
I'le befworne hee was a grande iurie man in refpect of me,
thofe graybeard Huddle-duddles and crufty cum-twangs,
were ftrooke with fuch ftinging remorfe of their miferable
Euclionifme and fundgery, that hee was not yet cold in his
graue but they challenged him to be borne amongft them,
and they and fixe cities more, entred a fharpe warre aboute
it, euery one of them laying claime to him as their owne,
and to this effect hath Bucchanan an Epigram.

   Urbes certarunt feptem de patria Homeri,
   Nulla domus viuo patria nulla fuit.
Seauen citties ftroaue whence *Homer* firft fhoulde come
When liuing, he no country had nor home.

I alleadge this tale to fhewe howe much better my lacke

then *Homers* (though all the King of Spaines Indies will not
create me ſuch a nigling Hexameter-founder as he was)in
the firſt proclayming of my banke-rout indigence and beg-
gery, to bende my courſe to ſuch a curteous compaſſionate
clime as Yarmouth,and to warne others that aduaunce their
heades aboue all others, and haue not reſpected, but rather
flatly oppoſed themſelues againſt the Frier medicants of our
profeſſion,what their amercements and vnrepriueable pen-
nance will be, excepte they teare ope their oyſtermouthd
pouches quickly,and make double amendes for their parſi-
mony. I am no *Tireſias* or *Calchas* to prophecie, but yet I
cannot tell,there may bee more reſounding bel-mettall in
my pen then I am aware,and if there bee, the firſt peale of it
is Yarmouthes. For a patterne or tiny-ſample what my ela-
borate performance would bee in this caſe, had I a ful-ſayld
gale of proſperity to encourage mee, whereas at the diſhu-
mored compoſing hereof may iuſtly complaine with *Ouid,*
Anchora iam noſtram non tenet vlla ratem.

My ſtate is ſo toſt and weather-beaten that it hath
nowe no anchor-holde left to cleaue vnto. I care not,if in a
dimme farre of launce-ſkippe, I take the paines to deſcribe
this ſuperimente principall Metropolis of the redde Fiſh. A
towne it is that in rich ſituation exceedeth many citties,and
without the which, *Caput gentis,* the ſwelling Battlementes
of Gurguntus,a head citty of Norffolke,and Suffolke,would
ſcarce retaine the name of a Citty , but become as ruinous
and deſolate as Thetforde or Ely : out of an hill or heape of
ſande, reared and enforced from the ſea moſt miraculouſly,
and by the ſingular pollicy and vnceſſant ineſtimable ex-
pence of the Inhabitantes, ſo firmely piled and rampierd a-
gainſt the furniſh waues battry,or ſuyng the leaſte action of
recouerie,that it is more coniecturall of the twaine,the land
with a writ of a *Eiectione firma* wil get the vpperhande of the
Ocean,then the Ocean one crowes ſkip preuaile againſt the
Continent. Forth of the ſands thus ſtruglingly as it exalteth
and

and liftes vp his glittering head. So of the neyboring fands
no leſſe femblably (whether in recordation of their worn
out affinitie or no,I know not) it is ſo inamorately protected
and patronized, that they ſtand as a trench or guarde about
it in the night,to keep off their enemies. Now in that drow-
fie empire of the pale-fac't Queene of ſhades,malgre letting
driue vpon their Barricadoes, or impetuouſly contending to
breake through their chaine or barre,but they entombe and
baliſt with ſodaine deſtruction. In this tranſcurſiue reporto-
ry without ſome obſeruant glaunce, I may not dully ouer-
paſſe the gallant beauty of their hauen, which hauing but as
it were a welte of land, or as M.Camden cals it,*lingulam ter-*
re, a little tong of the earth betwixte it and the wide Maine,
ſticks not to mannage armes, and hold his owne vndefeaſa-
bly againſt that vniuerſall vnbounded empery of ſurges,and
ſo hath done for this hundreth yeere. Two mile in length it
ſtretched his winding current, and then meetes with a ſpati-
ous riuer or backwater that feedes it. A narrow channell or
Iſthmus in raſh view you woulde opinionate it : when this I
can deuoutly auerre , I beholding it with both my eies this
laſt fiſhing,ſixe hundreth reaſonable barkes and veſſelles of
good burden (with a vantage) it hath giuen ſhelter to at
once in her harbour,and moſt of them riding abreſt before
the Key betwixt the Bridge and the Southgate. Many bows
length beyond the marke,my penne roues not I am certain,
if I doe,they ſtand at my elbow that can correct mee. The
delectableſt luſtie ſight and mouingeſt obiect, me thought
it was that our Ile ſets forth,and nothng behinde in number
with the inuincible *Spaniſh Armada*, though they were not
ſuch Gargantuan boyſterous gulliguts as they,though ſhips
and galeaſſes they would haue beene reckoned in the nauy
of K.*Edgar*,who is chronicled& regiſtred with three thoufand ſhips of warre to haue ſcoured the narrow ſeas, and ſailed round about England euery Summer. That which eſpe-
ciallelſt nouriſht the moſt prime pleaſure in me, was after a
ſtorme

storme when they were driuen in swarmes, and lay close pestred together as thicke as they could packe ; the next day following, if it were faire, they would cloud the whole skie with canuas, by spreading their drabled sailes in the full clue abroad a drying, and make a brauer shew with them, then so many banners and streamers displayed against the Sunne on a mountaine top. But how Yarmouth of it selfe so innumerable populous and replenished, and in so barraine a plot seated, should not onely supply her inhabitants with plentifull purueyance of sustenance, but prouant and victuall moreouer this monstrous army of strangers, was a matter that egregiously bepuzled and entranced my apprehension. Hollanders, Zelanders, Scots, French, Westerne men, Northren men, besides all the hundreds and wapentakes nine miles compasse, fetch the best of their viands and mangery from her market. For ten weeks together this rabble rout of outlandishers are billetted with her, yet in all that while the rate of no kinde of food is raised, nor the plenty of their markets one pinte of butter rebated, aud at the ten weekes end, when the campe is broken vp, no impression of any dearth left, but rather more store then before. Some of the towne dwellers haue so large an opinion of their setled prouision, that if all her Maiesties fleet at once should put into their bay, within twelue dayes warning with so much double beere, beefe, fish and bisket they would bulke them as they could wallow away with.

Here I could breake out into a boundlesse race of oratory, in shrill trumpetting and concelebrating the royall magnificence of her gouernement, that for state and strict ciuill ordering, scant admitteth any riuals : but I feare it would be a theame displeasant to the graue modesty of the discreet present magistrates; and therefore consultiuely I ouerslip it, howsoeuer I purpose not in the like nice respect to leape ouer the laudable petigree of Yarmouth, but will fetch her from her swadling clouts or infancy, & reueale to you when

and

and by whom fhe was firft raught out of the oceans armes, and ftart vp and afpired to fuch ftarry fublimitie, as alfo acquaint you with the notable immunities, franchifes, priuileges fhe is endowed with beyond all het confiners, by the difcentine line of kings from the conqueft.

There be of you it may be, that will accountme a paltrer, for hanging out the figne of the redde Herring in my title page, and no fuch feaft towards for ought you can fee. Soft and faire my maifters, you muft walke and talke before dinner an houre or two, the better to whet your appetites to tafte of fuch a dainty difh as the redde Herring, and that you may not thinke the time tedious, I care not if I beare you company, and leade you a found walke round about Yarmouth, and fhew you the length and bredth of it.

The mafters and batchellours commenfement dinners at Cambridge and Oxford, are betwixt three and foure in the afternoone, & the reft of the antecedence of the day worne out in difputations : imagine this the act or commenfement of the red Herring, that proceedeth batcheler, mafter & doctor all at once, & therefore his difputations muft be longer. But to the point, may it pleafe the whole generation of my auditours to be aduertifed, how that noble earth where the town of great Yarmouth is now mounted, & where fo much fifh is fold, in the dayes of yore, hath bin the place where you might haue catch fifh, & as plaine a fea within this 600. yere as any bote could tumble in, & fo was the whole leuill of the Marfhes betwixt it and Norwich. *An. Do.* 1000. or thereabouts (as I haue fcrapt out of wormeaten Parchment) and in the Raigne of *Canutus*, hee that dyed drunke at Lambeth or Lome-hith, fomewhat before, or fomewhat after, not a prenticefhip of yeares varying : *Caput extulit vndis*, the fands fet vp fhop for themfelues, and from that moment to this fextine centurie (or let me not be taken with a lye, fiue hundred nintie eight, that wants but a paire of yeares to make me a true man) they would no more liue vnder the

yoke

yoke of the Sea , or haue their heads waſht with his bubbly
ſpume or Barbers balderdaſh, but clearely quitted, diſter-
minated and relegated themſelues from his inflated Capri-
ciouſneſſe of playing the Dictator ouer them.

The Northerne winde was the clanging trumpetter,
who with the terrible blaſt of his throate , in one yeallow
heape or plumpe cluſtred or congeſted them togither, euen
as the Weſterne gales in Holland right ouer againſt them,
haue wrought vnruly hauocke, and threſht and ſwept the
ſandes ſo before them, that they haue choakt or claimd vp
the middle walke or dore of the *Rhene* , and made it as ſta-
ble a clod-mould, or turffe ground, as any hedger can driue
ſtake in. Caſter two mile diſtant from this new Yarmouth
we intreate of, is inſcribed to be that olde Yarmouth, wherof there are ſpecialties to be ſeene in the oldeſt writers , and
yet ſome viſible apparant tokens remaine of a hauen that ran
vp to it, and there had his entrance into the ſea, by aged Fiſhermen commonly tearmed *Grubs Hauen*) though now it
be graueld vp, and the ſtreame or tyde-gate turned another
way. But this is moſt warrantable, the *Alpha* of all the Yar-
mouths it was, & not the *Omega* correſpondently, & frō her
withered roote they branch the high aſcent of their genea-
logie. *Omnium rerum viciſſitudo eſt,* ones falling , is anothers
riſing , and ſo fell it out with that ruind Dorpe or hamlet,
which after it had relapſt into the Lordes handes for want of
reparations, and there were not men enough in it to defend
the ſhore from inuaſion, one *Cerdicus* a Plaſhing Saxon ,
that had reueld here and there with his battleaxe, on the
bordring bankes of the decrepite ouerworne village now
ſurnamed *Gorlſtone* threw forth his anchor , and with the af-
ſiſtance of his ſpeare, in ſtead of a pikeſtaffe, leapt agroūd like
a ſturdie bruite, and his yeomen bolde caſt their heeles in
their necke, and friskt it after him, and thence ſprouteth that
obſcene appellation of *Sarding ſandes* , with the draffe of
the

the carterly Hoblobs thereabouts, concoct or difgeaft for a
fcripture, verity, when the right chriftendome of it, is Cerdicke fands, or Cerdick fhore, of Cerdicus fo denominated,
who was the firft maylord or captaine of the morris daunce
that on thofe embenched fhelues ftampt his footing, where
cods & dogfifh fwomme net a warp of weeks forerunning)
& til he had giuen the onfet, they balkt thē as quickfands. By
and by after his iumping vppon them, the Saxons for that
Garianonum, or Yarmoth that had giuen vp the ghoft, in
thofe flymie plafhie fieldes of Gorfftone trowled vp a fecond Yarmouth, abutting on the Weft fide of the fhore of
this great Yarmouth, that is, but feeling the ayre to be vn-
holfome and difagreeing with them, to the ouerwhart brink
or verge of the flud, that writ all one ftile of Cerdicke fands,
they diflodged with bagge and baggage, and there layde
the foundatiō of a third Yarmouth *Quam nulla poteft abolere
vetuftas,* that I hope will holde vp her head till Doomefday.
In this Yarmouth as Mafter *(amden* faith, there were fea-
uentie inhabitants, or houfholders, that payed fcot and lot
in the time of *Edward* the Confeffor, but a Chronography-
cal Latine table, which they haue hanging vp in their Guild
hall, of all their tranfmutations from their Cradlehoode, in-
fringeth this a little, and flatters her, fhee is a great deale
yonger, in a faire text hand texting vnto vs, how in the Scep-
terdome of *Edward* the Confeffor, the fands firft began to
growe into fight at a low water, and more fholder at the
mouth of the ryuer *Hirus* or *Ierus*, whereupon it was dub-
bed Iernmouth or Yarmouth, and then there were two
Channels, one on the North, another on the South, where
through the fifher-men did wander and wauer vp to Norwitch, and diuers parts of Suffolke and Norfolke, all the fen-
nie *Lerna* betwixt, that with Reede is fo imbriftled, being
(as I haue forefpoke or fpoken to fore) *Madona, Amphi-
trite,* fluctuous demeans or fee fimple.

From the Citie of Norwich on the Eaft part, it is fixteene
mile

mile diſiunct, and diſlorated, and though betwixt the Sea
and the ſalt flud it be interpoſed, yet in no place about it can
you digge ſixe foote deepe, but you ſhall haue a guſhing
ſpring offreſh or ſweete water for all vſes, as apt and accom-
modate, as Saint Winifrides Well, or Towre-hill water at
London, ſo much praiſed and ſought after. My Tables are
not yet one quarter emptied of my notes out of their Table,
which becauſe it is, as it were a Sea Rutter diligently kept
amongſt them from age to age, of all their ebbs and flowes,
and winds that blew with or againſt them, I tie my ſelfe to
more preciſely, and thus it leadeth on.

In the time of King *Herrolde* and *William* the Conquerour, this ſand of Yarmouth grew to a ſetled lumpe, and was
as drie as the ſands of Arabia, ſo that thronging theaters of
people (as well Aliens as Engliſhmen) hiued thither about
the ſelling of fiſh and Herring, from Saint Michael to Saint
Martin, and there built ſutlers booths and tabernacles, to
canopie their heads in from the rhewme of the heauens, or
the clouds diſſoluing Cataracts. King *William Rufus* hauing
got the Golden wreath about his head, one *Herbertus* Bi-
ſhop of the ſea of Norwich, hearing of the gangs of good
fellowes, that hurtled and buſtled thither, as thicke as it had
beene to the ſhrine of Saint *Thomas* a *Becket*, or our Ladie
of Walſingham, builded a certaine Chappell there for the
ſeruice of God, and ſaluation of ſoules.

In the raigne of King *Henrie* the firſt, King *Steuen*, King
Henrie the ſecond, and *Richard de corde Lyon*, the apoſta-
cie of the ſands from the yalping world was ſo great, that
they ioynd themſelues to the maine land of Eaſtſlege, and
whole tribes of males and females, trotted bargd it thither
to build and enhabite, which the ſaide Kinges whil-s they
weilded their ſwords temporall animaduertiſed of, aſſigned
a ruler or gouernour ouer them, that was called the Kings
prouoſt, and that manner of prouoſtſhip or gouernment remained in full force and vertue all their fowre Throneſhips,
Alias

Alias a hundred yeare, euen till the inanguration of King *Iohn*, in whose dayes the forewritten-of Bishop of Norwich, seeing the numbrous increase of soules of both kindes that there had framd their nests, and meant not to forsake them till the soule Bell towld them thence, puld downe his Chappell, and what by himselfe and the deuout oblations and donatines of the fishermen vpon euery returne with their nets full, reedifide and rayfed it to a Church of that magnitude, as vnder ministers and Cathedrals verie queasie it admits any haylefellow well met, and the Church of Saint Nicholas he hallowed it, whence Yarmuouth roade is nicknamed the Roade of Saint Nicholas. King *Iohn* to comply and keep confort with his aunceltors in furthring of this new waterworke, in the ninth yeare of the engirting his annoynted browes with the refulgent Ophir circle, and Anno 1 2 0 9. set a fresh glosse vppon it, of the towne or free burrough of Yarmouth, and furnisht it with many substantial priuiledges and liberties, to haue and to holde the same of him, and his race, for fifty fiue pound yearely. In *Anno 1 2 4 0.* it percht vp to be gouernd by balies, and in a narrower limmitte then the forty yeares vndermeale of the seauen sleepers, it had so much towe to her diftaffe and was so well lined and bumbafted, that in a sea battell her shippes and men conflicted the cinque ports, and therein so laid about them, that they burnt, tooke, and spoyled the most of them, whereof such of them as were sure flights, (sauing a reuerence of their manhoods) ranne crying and complayning to King *Henry* the second, who with the aduice of his counsaile, set a fine of a thousand pound on the Yarmouth mens heads for that offence, which fine in the tenth of his reigne hee dispenc't with and pardoned.

Edward the first, and Edward the second likewise, let them lacke for no priuiledges, changing it from a burrough to a porte towne, and there setting vp a custome house with the appurtenances for the loading and vnloading of ships,

Henry

Henry the third in the fortieth of his empery cheard vp their blouds with two charters more, and in *Anno 1262*. and forty fiue of his courſe keeping, hee permitted them to wall in their towne, and moate it about with a broade ditch, and to haue a priſon or iaile in it. In the ſwindge of his trident, he conſtituted two Lord admirals ouer the whole nauy of England, which he diſpoſed in two partes, the one to beare ſway from the thames mouth Northwarde, called the Northren nauy, the other to ſhape his courſe from the thames mouth to the weſtwarde termed the weſterne nauy, and ouer this northren nauy, for admirall commiſſionated one Iohn Peerbrowne burgeſſe of the towne of Yarmouth, and ouer the weſterne nauy one Sir Robert Laburnus knight.

But Peerebrowne did not only hold his office all the time of that king doeing plauſible ſeruice, but was againe Readmirald by Edward the third and ſo died; in the fourteenth of whoſe raigne, he met with the french Kinges nauy, beeing foure-hundred ſaile, neere to the hauen of *Sluſe*, and there ſo ſlic't and ſlaſht them & tore their plancks to mammocks, and their leane guttes to kites meate, that their beſt mercy was fire & water which hath no mercie, and not a victuelar or a drumbler of them hanging in the winde aloofe, but was rib-roaſted or had ſome of his ribbes cruſht with their ſton-darting engines, no ordinance then beeing inuented. This Edward the thirde of his propenſiue minde towardes them, vnited to Yarmouth Kirtley roade, from it ſeauen mile vacant, and ſowing in the furrowes that his predeceſſours had entred, hayned the price of their priuiledges & not brought them downe one barley kirnell.

Richard the ſecond, vpon a diſcord twixt Leyſtofe and Yarmouth, after diuerſe law-dayes and arbitrarie mandates to the counties of Suffolke and Norfolke directed about it, in proper perſon 1385. came to Yarmouth, and in his parliamente the yeare enſuing, confirmed vnto it the liberties of Kirtley roade, (the onely motiue of all their contention).

Henrie

Henrie the fifth or the fifth of the Henries that ruled ouer vs, abridged them not a mite of their purchaſt prerogatiues, but permitted them to builde a bridge ouer their hauen and ayded and furthered them in it. Henry the ſixth, Edward the fourth, Henry the ſeauenth and King Henry the eight, with his daughters Queene Mary and our *Chara deum ſoboles* Queene Elizabeth, haue not withred vp their handes in ſigning and ſubſcribing to their requeſts, but our virgin rectoreſſe moſt of al, hath ſhoured downe her bounty vpon them, graunting them greater graunts then euer they had, beſides by-matters of the clarke of the marketſhippe, and many other beneuolences towardes the reparation of their porte. This and euery towne hath his backewinters or froſtes that nippe it in the blade (as not the cleareſt ſunne-ſhine but hath his ſhade, and there is a time of ſicknes as well as of health) The backewinter, the froſte biting, the eclipſe, or ſhade, and ſickneſſe of Yarmouth was, a greate ſickneſſe or plague in it 1348, of which in one yeare ſeauen thouſand and fifty people toppled vp their heeles there. The newe building at the weſt ende of the Church was begunne there 1330, which like the imperfit workes of kinges colledge in Cambridge, or Chriſt-church in Oxford, haue too coſtly large foundations to be euer finiſhed,

It is thought if the towne had not beene ſo ſcourged and eaten vp by that mortality, out of their owne purſes they woulde haue proceeded with it, but nowe they haue gone a neerer way to the woode, for with wooden galleries in the Church that they haue, and ſtayry degrees of ſeates in them, they make as much roome to ſitte and heare, as a newe weſt end would haue done.

The length and bredth of Yarmouth I promiſed to ſhew you; haue with you, haue with you : but firſt looke wiſtly vpon the walles, which if you marke, make a ſtretcht out quadrangle with the hauen. They are in compaſſe from the

South

South cheanes to the North cheanes, two thousand one hundreth and fourescore yardes. They haue towres vpon them sixteene : mounts vnderfonging & enflancking them two of olde, now three, which haue their thundring tooles to compell *Deigo Spanyard* to ducke, and strike the winde collicke in his paunch, if he praunce to neere them, and will not vaile to the Queene of England. The compasse about the wall of this new mount is fiue hundreth foot, and in the measure of yards eight score and seuen. The bredth of the foundation nine foot : the depth within ground eleuen. The heighth to the setting thereof fifteene foot, and in bredth at the setting of it, fiue foot three inches, and the procerous stature of it (so embailing and girdling in this mount) twentie foot and sixe inches. Gates to let in her friends, and shut out her enemies, Yarmouth hath ten lans, seuenscore: as for her streets, they are as long as threescore streets in London, and yet they diuide them but into three. Voide ground in the towne from the walles to the houses, and from the houses to the hauen, is not within the verge of my Geometry. The liberties of it on the fresh water one way, as namely from Yarmouth to *S. Toolies* in Beckles water, are ten mile, and from Yarmouth to Hardlie crosse another way, ten mile, and conclusiuely, from Yarmouth to Waybridge in the narrow North water tenne mile; in all which foords or *Meandors*: none can attache, arrest, distresse, but their officers; and if any drowne themselues in them, their Crowners sit vpon them.

I had a crotchet in my head, here to haue giuen the raines to my pen, and run astray thorowout all the coast townes of England, digging vp their dilapidations, and raking out of the dust-heape or charnell house of tenebrous eld, the rottenest relique of their monuments, and bright scoured the canker eaten brasse of their first bricklayers and founders, & commented and paralogized on their condition in the present, & in the pretertense, not for any loue or hatred I beare

them,

them, but that I would not be fnibd, or haue it caſt in my
diſhe, that therefore I prayſe Yarmouth ſo rantantingly, becauſe I neuer elſewhere bayted my horſe, or tooke my bowe
and arrowes and went to bed. Which leeſing (had I bene
let alone) I would haue put to bed with a recumbentibus,
by vttering the beſt, that with a ſafe conſcience mought
be vttred of the beſt, or worſt of them all, and notwithſtan-
ding all at beſt, that tongue could ſpeake, or hart could
thinke of them, they ſhould bate me an ace of Yarmouth.
Mutch brainetoſſing and breaking of my ſcull it coſt me,
but farewell it, and farewel the Baylies of the Cynqueports,
whoſe primordiat *Gethneliaca*, was alſo dropping out of my
inckhorne, with the ſyluer oare of their barronry by *William*
the Conquerour conueyed ouer them at that nicke when
hee firmed and rubrickt the Kentiſhmens gauill kinde of the
ſonne to inherite at fifteene, and the felony of the father not
to draw a foot of land from the ſonne, & amongſt the ſonnes
the portion to be equally diſtributed; and if there were no
ſonnes, much good doe it the daughters, for they were to
ſhare it after the ſame tenure, and might alienate it how they
would, either by legacy or bargaine without the conſent of
the lord.

To ſhun ſpight, I ſmothered theſe dribblements, & refrai-
ned to deſcant how *William* the Conquerour hauing heard
the prouerbe of Kent and Chriſtendome, thought he had
woonne a countrey as good as all Chriſtendome, when he
was enfeofed of Kent, for which, to make it ſure vnto him
after he was entailed thereunto, nought they askt they nee-
ded to aske twiſe, it being enacted ere the words came out
of their mouth. Of that profligated labour, yet my breaſt
pants and labours : a whole moneths minde of reuoluing
meditation, I raueling out therein (as raueling out ſignifies
Penelopes telam retexere, the vnweauing of a webbe before
wouen and contexted:) It pities me, it pities me, that in cutting of ſo faire a diamond as Yarmouth, I haue not a casket

duſky

duſky Coruiſh diamonds by me, and a boxe of muddy foiles the better to ſet it forth. *Ut nemo miſer niſi comparatus, ſic nihil pro mirifico niſi cum alijs conferatur. Cedite ſoli ſtellæ ſcintillan-tes, ſoli Garrianano cedite reliqua oppida veligera ſedium naualium ſpeciociſſimo ſed redeo ad vernaculum.*

All Common wealths aſſume their prenominations of their common diuided weale, as where one man hath not too much riches, and another man too much pouertie: Such was *Platos* communitie and *Licurgus*, and the olde Romans lawes, of meaſuring out their fields, their meads, their paſtures & houſes, and meating out to euery one his childes portion. To this *Commune bonum* (or euery horſe his loafe) Yarmouth in propinquity is as the buckle to the thong, and the next finger to the thumbe; not that it is ſibbe or cater-couſins to any mūgrel *Democratia*, in which one is all, & all is one, but that in her as they are not al one ſo one or two there pockets not vp all the peeces, there beeing two hundreth in it worth three hundred pounde a peece, with poundage and ſhillings to the lurtched, ſet a ſide the Bailifes fowre and twentie, and eight and fourtie. Put out mine eye, who can with ſuch another bragge of my Sea towne within two hundred myle of it. But this common good within it ſelfe, is nothing to the common good it communicats to the whole ſtate. Shall I particularize vnto you, *quibus vijs & modis*, how and wherein. There is my hand to, I will doe it, and this is my *Exordium*. A towne of defence it is to the Counties of Suffolke and Norfolke againſt the enemies, (ſo acounted at the firſt graunting of their liberties) and by the naturall ſtrength of the ſituation ſo apparant, being both inuironed with many ſands, and now of late by great charge, much more fortified then in auncient times. All the Realme it profiteth many waies, as by the free Faire of herring chiefly, maintained by the fiſher-men of Yarmouth themſelues, by the great plentie of ſalted fiſh there, not ſo little two yeares paſt as foure hundred thouſand, wherein were imployed

about

about fourescore saile of barkes of their owne.

By the furnishing forth of forty boates for mackerell at the spring of the yeare when all thinges are dearest, which is a great reliefe to all the country thereaboutes, and soone after Bartlemewe-tyde, a hundred and twenty sayle of their owne for herrings, and forty sayle of other ships and barkes trading Newe castle, the lowe countries and other voyages. Norwitch at her Maiesties comming in progresse thither, presented her with a shew of knitters on a high stage placed for the nonce, Yarniouth if the like occasiō were, could clap vp as good a shewe of netbrayders, or those that haue no cloathes to wrappe their hides in or breade to put in their mouthes, but what they earne and get by brayding of nets, (not so little as two thousand pound they yearely disperfing amongst the poore women and children of the country, for the spinning of twine to make them with, besides the labour of the enhabitauntes in working them) and for a cōmodious greene place neere the seashoare to mende and drie them, not Salsbury plaine or Newmarket heath (though they haue no vicinity or neighbourhoode with the sea, or scarce with any ditch or pond of freshwater) may ouerpeere or out crow her, there being aboue fiue thousand pounds worth of them at a time vppon her dennes a sunning. A conuenient key within her hauen shee hath, for the deliuery of nets and herrings, where you may lie a floate at a lowe water; (I beseech you doe not so in the thames), many seruiceable marriners and seafaring-men shee trayneth vp (but of that in the herring.)

The marishes and lower grounds lying vpon the three riuers that vagary vp to her, (comprehending many thousand acres) by the vigilant preseruation of their hauen are encreafed in value more then halfe, which else would be a *Mæotis palus*, a meare or lake of Eeles Frogges, and wilde-duckes. The citty of Norwitch (as in the *Preludium* heereof I had a twitch at) fares were the worse for her, nor would fare so wel

D

if it were not for the fiſhe of all ſortes that ſhee cloyeth her
with, and the felowſhip of their hauen into which their three
riuers infuſe themſelues, and through which their goods and
merchandiſe from beyonde ſeas are keeled vp with ſmall
coſt to their very threſholds, and to many good townes on
this ſide, and beyond. I woulde be loth to builde a laborinth
in the gatehouſe of my booke, for you to looſe your ſelues
in, and therefore I ſhred of many thinges, we will but caſt o-
uer the bill of her charge, and talke a worde or two of her
buildings, and breake vp and go to breakefaſt with the red
herring. The hauen hath coſt in theſe laſt 28. yeares, ſixe
and twenty thouſand two hundred and ſixe and fifty pounde
foure ſhillinges and fiue pence. Fortification and poulder
ſince *Anno 1587.* two thouſand markes, the ſea-ſeruice in
Anno 1588. eight hundreth poundes, the Portingale voyage a thouſand pound, the voyage to Cales as much.

It hath loſt by the Dunkerkers a thouſand pound, by the
Frenchmen three thouſand, by Wafting eight hundred, by
the Spaniardes and other loſſes not rated, at the leaſt three
thouſand more . The continuall charge of the Towne in
maintenance of their Hauen, fiue hundred pounds a yeare,
Omnibus annis for euer, the feefarme of the Towne fiftie fiue
pound, and fiue pound a yeare aboue for Kirtley Roade. The
continuall charge of the bridge ouer the hauen, their walls,
and a number of other odde reckonings we deale not with,
towards all which they haue not in certaine reuenewes a-
boue fiftie or three-ſcore pounds a yeare, and that is in houſes. The yearely charge towards the prouiſion of fiſhe for
her Maieſtie 1000. pounds, as for arable matters of tillage
and husbandrie, and graſing of cattell, their barraine ſands
will not beare them , and they get not a beggers noble by
one or other of them, but their whole harueſt is by Sea.

It were to be wiſhed that other coaſters were ſo induſtri-
ous as the Yarmouth, in winning the treaſure of fiſh out of
thoſe profundities, and then we ſhould haue twentie egges
a penny

a pennie : and it would be as plentifull a world as when Abbies ftoode : and now if there be any plentifull world, it is in Yarmouth. Her fumptuous porches and garnifht buildings are fuch, as no port Towne in our Brittifh circumference (nay, take fome porte Citties ouer-plus into the bargain(r) may fuitably ftake with, or adequate.

By the proportion of the Eaft furprifed Gades or Cales, diuers haue tried their cunning, to configurate a twinlike image of it, both in the correlatiue analagie of the fpanbroad rowle running betwixt, as alfo of the skirt or lappet of earth whereon it ftands, heerein onely limitting the difference, that the houfes heere are not fuch flatte cuftard Crownes at the top as they are. But I for my parte caft it afide as two obfcure a Canton, to demonftrate and take the altitude by of fo *Elizian* a habitation as Yarmouth. Of a bounzing fidewalted parifh in Lancafhire, we haue a flying voyce difperfed, where they goe nine mile to Church euery Sunday, but Parifh for Parifh throughout Lancafhire, Chefhire, or Wingandecoy, both for numbers in groffe of honeft houfhoulders, youthfull couragious valiant fpirites, and fubftantiall graue Burgers, Yarmouth fhall droppe vie with them to the laft *Edward* groate they are worth. I am polting to my propofed fcope, or elfe I could runne tenne quier of paper out of breath, in further trauerfing her rightes and dignities.

But of that ftaught I muft not take in two liberall, in cafe I want ftowage for my red Herring, which I rely vpon as my wealthieft loading. Farewell flourifhing Yarmouth, and be euery day more flourifhing then other vntill the latter day, whiles I haue my fence or exiftence, I will perfift in louing thee, and fo with this abrupt *Poft fcript* I leaue thee. I haue not trauaild farre, though conferred with fartheft trauailers, from our owne Realme, I haue turnd ouer venerable *Bede,* and plenteous beadrowles of frierly annals following on the backe of him . *Polidore Virgill, Bucchanan, Camdens Brittania* and moft recordes of friendes, or enemies I haue

fearcht

searcht as concerning the later modell of it, none of the inland partes thereof but I haue traded them as frequently as the middle walke in Poules, or my way to bed euery night, yet for ought I haue read, heard, or seene, Yarmouth regall Yarmouth of all maritimall townes that are no more but fisher townes soly raigneth sance peere.

Not any where is the word seuerer practised, the preacher reuerentlier obserued and honoured, iustice founder ministred, and a warlike people peaceablier demeanourd, betwixte this and the *Grand Cathay*, and the strand of *Prester Iohn.*

Adew adue, tenne thousand folde delicate paramour of *Neptune*, the nexte yeare my standish may haps to addresse another voyage vnto thee, if this haue any acceptace. Now it is high heaking time, and bee the windes neuer so easterly aduerse and the tyde fled from vs, wee must violently towe and hale in our redoubtable *Sophy* of the floating kingdom of *Pisces*, whome so much as by name I shoulde not haue acknowledged, had it not beene that I mused how Yarmouth should be inuested in such plenty and opulence, considering that in M. *Hackluits* English discoueries, I haue not come in ken of one mizzen mast of a man of warre bound for the Indies or mediteranean sternebearer sente from her *Zenith* or *Meridian*; Mercuriall brested M. *Harborne* alwaies accepted a rich sparke of eternity first lighted and enkindled at Yarmouth, or there first bred and brought forth to see the light, who since in the hottest degrees of *Leo*, hath ecchoing noysed the name of our Ilande and of Yarmouth so *Tritonly* that not an infant of the curtaild skinclipping pagans but talk of London as frequently as of their Prophets tombe at *Mæcha*, & as much worships or maidenpeace as it were but one sun that shin'd ouer them all . Our first embassadour was he to the *Behemoth* of *Constantinople*, and as *Moses* was sent from the omnipotent God of heauen to perswade with *Sultan Pharao* to let the children of Israell goe, so from the prepotent

potent goddeſſe of the earth *Eliza* was hee ſent to ſet free
the Engliſh captiues and open vnto vs the paſſage into the
redde ſea and *Euphrates*. How impetrable hee was in mol-
lyfying the * adamantineſt tiranny of mankinde, and houre- | * The adamāt
ly crucifier of *Ieſus Chriſt* crucifyde & wrooter vp of *Palle-* | mollifide with
ſtine thoſe that be ſcrutinus to pry into, let them reuolue the | nothing but
Digeſts of our Engliſh diſcoucries cited vp in the prece- | bloud.
dence,and be documentized moſt locupleatly. Of him and
none but him who in valuation is woorth 18. huge *Argoſees*
full of our preſent dated miſhapen childiſh trauailers,haue I
took ſent or come in the wind of,that euer Yarmoth vnſhel
led or ingendred to weather it on till they loſt the North-
ſtarre,or ſailed iuſt *Antipodes* againſt vs, nor walking in her
ſtreetes ſo many weekes togither could I meete with any of
theſe ſwaggering captaines, (captaines that wore a whole
antient in a ſcarfe which made them goe heaue ſhouldred it
was ſo boyſterous) or huſtituſtie youthfull ruffling com-
rades wearing euery one three yeardes of feather in his cap
for his miſtris fauour,ſuch as wee ſtumble on at each ſecond
ſtep at Plimmouth, Southampton , and Portſmouth, but an
eniuerſal marchantly formallity,in habitte,ſpeach, geſtures,
though little merchandiſe they beate their heades aboute,
Queene Norwitch for that goeing betweene them and
home,at length (ô that length of the full pointe ſpoiles me,
all gentle readers I beſeech you pardon mee) I fell a com-
muning herupon with a gentleman a familiar of miue,& he
eftſoones defined vnto mee that the redde herring was this
old *Ticklecob*, or *Magiſter fac totum*,that brought in the red
ruddocks and the grummeli ſeed as thicke as oatmeale, and
made Yarmouth for argent to put dowue the citty of *Ar-*
gentine. Doe but conuert ſaid hee the ſlendereſt twinckling
reflexe of your eie-ſight to this flinty ringe that engirtes it,
theſe towred walles,port-cullizd-gates and gorgeous archi-
tectures that condecorate and adorne it, and then perponder of the red herringes priority and preualence,who is the
D 3   onely

onely vnexhauſtible mine that hath raiſd and begot all this, and minutely to riper maturity foſters and cheriſheth it. The red herring alone it is that counteruailes the burdenſome detrimentes of our hauen, which euery twelue-month deuoures a Iuſtice of peace liuing, in weares and banckes to beate off the ſand and ouerthwart ledging and fencing it in; that defrayes all impoſitions and outwarde payments to her Maieſtie (in which Yarmouth giues not the wall to ſixe, though ſixeteene moath-eaten burgeſſe townes that haue dawbers and thatchers to their Mayors, challenge in parliament the vpper hand of it) and for the vaward or ſubburbes of my narration, that empals our ſage ſenatours or *Ephori,* in princely ſcarlet as pompous oſtentyue as the *Vinti quater* or Lady *Troynonant;* wherefore quoth he if there be in thee any whit of that vnquechable ſacred fire of *Appollo* (as al men repute) and that *Minerua* amongeſt the number of her heires hath addopted thee, or thou wilt commend thy muſe to ſempiternity, and haue images and ſtatutes erected to her after her vnſtringed ſilent interment and obſequies, rouze thy ſpirites out of this drowſie lethargy of mellancholly they are drencht in, and wreſt them vp to the moſt outſtretched ayry ſtraine of elocution to chaunt and carroll forth the *Alteza* an excelſitude of this monarchall fluddy *Induperator.*

Very tractable to this lure I was trained, and put him not to the full anniling of me with any ſound hammering perſuaſion, in that at the firſt fight of the top-gallant towers of Yarmouth, and a weeke before he had broken any of theſe words betwixt his teeth, my muſe was ardently inflamed to do it ſome right, and how to bring it about fitter I knew not; then in the praiſe of the red herring, whoſe proper ſoile and nurſery it is. But this I muſt giue you to wit, how euer I haue tooke it vpon me, that neuer ſince I ſpouted incke, was I of woorſe aptitude to goe thorow with ſuch a mighty March brewage as you expect, or temper you one right cup of that ancient wine of *Falernum* which would laſt fourty yeere, or

confe-

confecrate to your fame a perpetuall temple of the Pine-
trees of *Ida* which neuer rot. For befides the loud bellow-
ing prodigious flaw of indignation, ftird vp againft me in
my abfence and extermination from the vpper region of
our celeftiall regiment, which hath dung mee in a maner
downe to the infernall bottome of defolation, and fo trou-
bledly bemudded with griefe and care euery cell or organ-
pipe of my purer intellectuall faculties, that no more they
confort with any ingenuous playful merriments, of my note-
books and all books elfe here in the countrey I am berea-
ued, whereby I might enamell and hatch ouer this deuice
more artificially and mafterly, and attire it in his true orient
varnifh and tincture, wherefore heart and good wil, a workman is nothing without his tooles, had I my topickes by
me in ftead of my learned counfell to affift me, I might haps
marfhall my termes in better aray, and beftow fuch coftly
coquery on this *Marine magnifico* as you would preferre him
before tart and galingale, which *Chaucer* preheminenteft
encomionizeth aboue all iunquetries or confectionaries
whatfoeuer.

Now you muft accept of it as the place ferues, and in ftead
of comfittes and fugar to ftrewe him with, take well in worth
a farthing worth of flower to white him ouer and wamble
him in, and I hauing no great pieces to difcharge for his
ben-uenue, or welcomming in, with this volley of *Rhapfodies*
or fmall fhotte, he muft reft pacified, and fo *Ad rem*, fpurre
cutte through thicke and thinne, and enter the triumphall
charriot of the red herring.

H*Omer* of rats and frogs hath heroiqut it, other oaten pi-
pers after him in praife of the Gnat, the Flea, the Hafill
nut, the Grafhopper, the Butterflie, the Parrot, the Popiniay,
Phillip fparrow, and the Cuckowe; the wantonner fort of
them fing defcant on their miftris gloue, her ring, her fanne,
her looking glaffe, her pantofle, and on the fame iurie, I
might impannell *Iohannes Secundus*, with his booke of the

two hundred kinde of leiſes. Phyloſophers come ſneaking
in with their paradoxes of pouertie, impriſonment, death,
ſickeneſſe, baniſhment, and baldneſſe, and as buſie they are
aboute the bee, the ſtorke, the conſtant turtle, the horſe,
the dog, the ape, the aſſe, the foxe, and the ferret. Phyſiti-
ons deafen our eares with the *Honorificabilitudinitatibus* of
their heauenly *Panachaa* their ſoueraigne *Guiacum*, their
gliſters, their triacles, their mithridates of fortie ſeuerall
poyſons compacted, their bitter *Rubarbe*, and torturing
Stibium.

The poſterior Italian and Germane cornugraphers, ſticke
not to applaude and cannonize vnnaturall ſodomitrie, the
ſtrumpet errant, the goute, the ague, the dropſie, the ſciati-
ca, follie, drunckenneſſe, and *ſlouenry.* The *Galli Gallina-
cei*, or cocking French ſwarme euery piſſing while in their
primmer editions, *Imprimeda iour duy*, of the vnſpeakeable
healthfull condicibleneſſe of the *Gomorrian* great *Poeo*, a *Po-
co*, their true countriman euery inch of him, the preſcript
lawes of *Tennis* or *Balonne* (which is moſt of their gentle-
mens chiefe liuelyhoodes) the commoditie of hoarſenes,
bleare-eyes, ſcabd hams, threed-bare cloakes, potcht eggs,
and *Panados.* Amongſt our Engliſh harmonious calinos,
one is vp with the excellence of the browne bill and the long
bowe, another playes his prizes in print, in driuing it home
with all weapons in right of the noble ſcience of defence: a
third writes paſſing enamorately, of the nature of white-
meates, and iuſtifies it vnder his hand to be bought & ſould
euery where, that they exceede *Nectar*, & *Ambroſia*: a fourth
comes foorth with ſomething in prayſe of nothing: a fift of
an enflamed heale to copperſmithes hal, all to beerimes it of
the diuerſitie of red noſes, and the hierarchy of the noſe
magnificat. A ſixt, ſweeps behinde the dore all earthly fe-
licities, and makes Bakers maulkins of them, if they ſtand in
competencie with a ſtrong dozen of poyntes; marrie they
muſt be poyntes of the matter, you muſt conſider, whereof

of the formoſt codpiſſe poynt is the cranes prouerbe in pain-
ted clothes feare God, and obey the king, and the reſt ſome
haue tagges, and ſome haue none. A ſeuenth ſettes a *Tobacco* pipe in ſtead of a trumpet to his mouth, and of
that diuine drugge proclaimeth miracles. An eygth cap-
pers it vp to the ſpheares in commendation of daunſing.
A ninth, offers ſacrifice to the goddeſſe *Cloaca*, and diſportes
himſelfe very ſchollerly and wittilie aboute the reformation
of cloſe ſtooles and houſes of office, and ſpicing and embal-
ming their rancke intrailes, that they ſtincke not. A tenth,
ſettes forth remedies of *Toſted turnes* againſt famine.

To theſe I might wedge in *Cornelius* the brabantine, who
was felloniouſly ſuſpected in 87. for penning a diſcourſe of
Tuſtinockados, and a countrey gentleman of my acquaintance who is launching forth a treatiſe as bigge garbd as the
french *Academy* of the *Cornucopia* of a cowe and what an ad-
uantageable creature ſhee is, beyonde all the foure footed
rablement of *Herbagers* and graſſe champers, day nor night
that ſhee can reſt for filing and tampring aboute it) as alſo a
ſworne brother of his that ſo bebangeth poore paper in laud
of a bag-pudding as a ſwizer would not belieue it. Neither
of their *Decads* are yet ſtampt but eare midſummer tearme
they will be if their wordes bee ſure payment, and then tell
me if our Engliſh ſconſes be not right Sheffield or no.

See the Epiſtle
comemndato-
rie, before M.
Samuell Dani-
els tranſlatiō of
the Empreſes
of Paulus Ioui-
us-

The application of this whole catalogue of waſt authours
is no more but this, *Quot capita tot ſententiæ,* ſo many heades
ſo many whirlegigs, and if all theſe haue *Terlery-ginckt* it ſo
friuolouſly of they reckt not what I may *Cum gratia & priue-
ligio* pronounce it, that a red herring is wholſeſome in a fro-
ſty morning, and rake vp ſome fewe ſcattered ſillables together in the exornation and polliſhing of it. No more ex-
curſions and circumquaques but *Totaliter a appoſitum.*

That Engliſh marchandiſe is moſt precious which no
country can be without, if you aſke *Suffolke, Eſſex, Kent, Suſ-
ſex, or Lemſter, or Cotſwold,* what marchandiſe that ſhoulde

E   be,

bee,they will anſwere you it is the very ſame which *Polidore*
Virgill cals *Verè aureum vellus*,the true gólden fleece of our
woll and Engliſh cloth and nought elſe,other engrating vp-
land cormorants will grunt out it is *Grana paradiſi* our grain
or corne that is moſt ſought after . The Weſterners and
Northerners that it is lead tinne and iron.Butter and cheeſe,
butter and cheeſe ſaith the farmer,but frō euery one of theſe
I diſſent and wil ſtoutely bide by it,that to trowle in the caſh
throughout all nations chriſtendome there is no fellowe
to the red herring . The French Spaniſh and Italian haue
wool inough of their owne wherof they make cloth to ſerue
their turne,though it be ſomewhat courſer then ours. For
corne, none of the Eaſt parts bnt ſurpaſſeth vs, of leade and
tinne is the moſt ſcarſity in forraine dominions,and plenty
with vs, though they are not vtterly barraine of them. As
for iron about *Iſenborough* and other places of *Germany*,
they haue quadruple the ſtore that wee haue. As touching
butter and cheeſe the *Hollanders* cry by your leaue wee muſt
goe before you,and the *Tranſalpiners* with their lordly *Par-*
maſin, (ſo named of the citty of *Parma* in Italy where it is
firſt clout-cruſhed and made)ſhoulder in for the vpper hand
as hotly,when as of our appropriate glory of the red herring,
no region twixt the poles articke and antartick may can or
will rebate from vs one ſcruple.
  On no coaſt like ours is it caught in ſuch abundance, no
where dreſt in his right cue but vnder our Horizon; hoſted
roſted and toſted heere alone it is, and as well poudred and
ſalted as any Duchman would deſire. If you articulate with
me of the gaine or profit of it, without the which the newe
fangleſt raritie, that no body can boaſt of but our ſelues, after three dayes gazing is reuerſt ouer to children for babies
to play with, behold it is euery mans money from the King
to the Courtier; euery houſholder or goodman *Baltrop*,that
keepes a family in pay, calls for it as one of his ſtanding pro-
uiſions . The poorer ſort make it three parts of there ſuſte-
nanuce

nance, with it for his dinnier the patchedeſt *Leather piltche laboratho* may dine like a Spaniſh Duke, when the niggardlieſt mouſe of biefe will coſt him ſixpence . In the craft of catching or taking it, and ſmudging it. Marchant and chapmanable as it ſhould be, it ſets a worke thouſands, who liue all the reſt of the yeare gayly well, by what in ſome fewe weekes they ſcratch vp then, and come to beare office of Queſtman and Scauinger in the Pariſh where they dwell, which they could neuer haue done, but would haue begd or ſtarud with their wiues and brattes, had not this Captaine of the ſquamy cattell ſo ſtoode their good Lord and maſter: Carpenters, Ship wrights, makers of lines, roapes and cables, dreſſers of Hempe, ſpinners of thred, and net weauers it giues their handfuls to , ſets vp ſo many ſalt-houſes to make ſalt, and ſalt vpon ſalt; keepes in earnings the Cooper, the Brewer the Baker, and numbers of other people , to gill, waſh and packe it, and carrie it and recarrie it.

In exchange of it from other Countries they returne wine and Woades, for which is alwaies paide ready Golde, with ſalt, Canuas, Vitre, and a great deale of good traſh . Her Maieſties tributes and cuſtomes, this *Semper Auguſtus* of the Seas finnie freeholders, augmenteth & enlargeth vncountably, and to the encreaſe of Nauigation, for her ſeruice hee is no enemie.

Voiages of purchaſe or repriſals, which are now grown a common traffique , ſwallow vp and conſume more Saylers and Marriners then they breede , and lightly not a ſlop of a ropehaler they ſend forth to the Queenes ſhips, but hee is firſt broken to the Sea in the Herring mans Skiffe or Cockboate , where hauing learned to brooke all waters , and drinke as he can out of a tarrie Canne, and eate poore Iohn out of ſwuttie platters when he may get it without butter or muſtard, there is no ho with him but once hartned thus, hee will needes be a man of warre, or a *Tobacco* taker, and weare a ſiluer Whiſtle . Some of theſe for their haughtie climbing

come

come home with woodden legges and fome with none, but leaue body and all behinde, thofe that efcape to bring news, tell of nothing but eating Tallow and yong black-amores, of fiue and fiue to a Rat in euery meffe, and the fhip-boy to the tayle, of ftopping their nofes when they drunke ftinking water that came out of the pumpe of the fhip, and cutting a greafie buffe ierkin in tripes and broiling it for their dinners. Diuers Indian aduentures haue beene feafoned with direr mifhaps, not hauing for eight dayes fpace the quantity of a candles-end among eight fcore to greafe their lippes with, and landing in the end to feeke food, by the canibal Sauages they haue bene circumuented, and forced to yeeld their bodies to feed them.

Our mitred Archpatriarch *Leopald* herring exacts no fuch *Mufcouian vaffailage of his liegemen , though hee put them to their trumps other while, and fcuppets not his benificence into their mouthes with fuch frefhwater facility as *M. Afcham* in his Schoolemafter would imply. His wordes thefe in his cenfure vpon *Varro: Hee enters not* (fayth he)*into any great depth of eloquēce, but as one carried in a fmall low veffell by himfelfe very nigh the common fhore, not much vnlike the fifher men of Rie, or herring men of Yarmouth, who deferue by common mens opinion fmall commendation for any cunning failing at all.* Well, he was her Maiefties Schoolemafter, and a *S. Iohns* man in Cambridge, in which houfe once I tooke vp my inne for feuen yere together lacking a quarter and yet loue it ftill, for it is and euer was the fweeteft nurfe of knowledge in all that Vniuerfity. Therefore I will keepe faire quarter with him, and expoftulate the matter more tamely. *Memorandum non abuno*, I vary not a minnum from him, that in the captious myftery of Mounfieur herring low veffels will not giue their heads for the wafhing, holding their owne pell-mell in all weathers as roughly as vafter timber men, though not fo neere the fhore, as through ignorance of the coaft he foundeth, nor one man by himfelfe alone to

doe

* That is for a man to be his owne executioner, and at his Princes becke to go vp to the top of the rock, and thence throw himfelfe headlong. Fol.63.pag.2,

do euery thing,which is the opinion of one man by himfelfe
alone,and not beleeu'd of any other. Fiue to one if he were
aliue,I would beate againft him, fince one without fiue is as
good as none,to gouerne the moft egfhell fhallop that floa-
teth,and fpread her nets,and draw them in, As ftifly could
I controuert it with him about pricking his card fo badly in
Cape Norfolke or *Sinus Yarmouthienfis* and difcrediting our
countrymen for fhorecreepers, like thefe Colchefter oy-
ftermen,or whiting-mungers and fprot-catchers.Solyman
Herring woulde you fhoulde perfwade your felues is loftier
minded and keepeth more aloofe then fo,and thofe that are
his followers if they will feeke him where hee is,more then
common daunger they muft incurre in clofe driuing vnder
the fands which alternately or betwixt times when he is dif-
pofed to enfconfe himfelfe are his entrenehed Randevowe
or caftle of retiring, and otherwhile fortie or thrèefcoare
leagues in the roaring territory they are glad on their wodden horfes to poft after him,and fcoure it with their ethiope
pitchbordes till they be windleffe in his queft and purfuing.
Returning from waiting on him, haue with you to the *Adri-*
atique and abroade euery where far and neere to make port-
fale of their perfumed fmoaky commodities, and that toyle
rockt a fleepe they are for *Vltima Theule* the northfeas or *If-*
*land,*and thence yerke ouer that worthy *Pallamede don pedro*
*de linge,*and his worfhipfull nephew *Hugo Habberdine,* and a
trundle-taile tike or fhaugh or two, and towardes *Michel-*
mas fcud home to catch Herring againe. This argues they
fhoulde haue fome experience of nauigation, and are not
fuch *Halcyons* to builde their neaftes all on the fhoare as *M.*
Afcam fuppofeth.

Rie is one of the antient townes belonging to the cinque
ports yet limpeth cinque ace behinde Yarmouth,and it wil
fincke when Yarmouth rifeth, and yet if it were put in the
ballance againft Yarmouth, it woulde rife when Yarmouth
fincketh,and to ftand threfhing no longer about it,Rie is Ry

and

and no more but Rie and Yarmouth wheate compared with
it. Wherefore had he bene a right clarke of the market, he
would haue set a higher price on the one then the other, and
set that one of highest price aboue the other.

Those that deserue by common mens opinion small commendation for any cunning sailing at all, are not the Yar-
mouthers how euer there is a foule fault in the print escapt,
that curstly squinteth and leereth that way, but the bonnie
Northren cobbles of his countrey, with their Indian canaos
or boats like great beefe trayes or kneading troughs, firking
as flight swift thorow the glassy fieldes of *Thetis*, as if it were
the land of yce, and sliding ouer the boiling desert so early,
and neuer bruise one bubble of it, as though they contended
to out-strip the light-foot tripper in the *Metamorphisis*, who
would run ouer the ripe-bending eares of corne, and neuer
shed or perish one kirnell. No such yron-fisted *Ciclops* to
hew it out of the flint, and runne thorow any thing as these
frost-bitten crab-tree fac't lads spunne out of the hards of the
towe, which are Donsel herrings lackeys at Yarmouth euery
fishing.

Let the carreeringest billow confesse and absolue it selfe,
before it pricke vp his bristles against them, for if it come vpon his dancing horse, and offer to tilt it with them, they will
aske no trustier lances then their oares to beat out the brains
of it, and stop his throat from belching.

These rubbes remooued, on with our game as fast as wee
may, & to the gaine of the red herring againe another crash.
Item if it were not for this *Huniades* of the liquid element,
that word *Quadragesima*, or Lent might be cleane spung'd
out of the Kalender, with Rogation weeks, Saints eues, and
the whole Ragmans roule of fasting dayes, and Fishmon-
gers might keepe Christmasse all the yeere, for any ouerla-
uish takings they should haue of clownes and clouted shoes,
and the rubbish menialty their best customers, and their
bloudy aduersaries the butchers would neuer leaue clea-
uing

uing it out in the whole chines, till they had got a Lord
Maior of their company as well as they. Nay out of their
wits they would be haunted with continuall takings, & stand
crosse-gag'd with kniues in their mouthes from one Shroft-
tuisday to another, and weare candles-endes in their hattes
at midsommer, hauing no time to shaue their prickes, or
washe their flyeblowne aprons if *Domingo Rufus* or *Sacra-
pant herring* caused not the dice to runne contrary.

The Rhomish rotten *Pithagoreans* or *Carthusian* friers,
that mumpe on nothing but fishe, in what a flegmatique
predicament would they be, did not this counterpoyson of
the spitting sickenesse (sixtiefolde more restoratiue then *Be-
zer*) patch them out and preserue them, which being dub-
ble rosted and dryde as it is, not onely sucks vp all rhewma-
tique inundations, but is a shooing-horne for a pinte of
wine ouer-plus.

The sweete smacke that Yarmouth findes in it, and how
it hath made it *Lippitudo Atticæ* (as it was saide of *Ægina* her
neere adiacent comfronter) the blemish and staine of all her
salt-water sisters in England, and multiplide it from a moul-
hill of sand, to a cloude-crowned mount *Teneriffe*, abbreui-
atly and meetely according to my old *Sarum* plaine song I
haue harpt vpon, and that, if there were no other certificat
or instance of the inlinked consanguinitie twixt him and
Lady Lucar, is *Instar mille*, worth a million of witnesses, to
exemplifie the ritches of him. The Poets were triuiall, that
set vp *Helens* face for such a top-gallant Summer May-pole
for men to gaze at, and strouted it out so in their buskind
braues of her beautie, whereof the onely *Circes Heypasse*, and
Repasse was that it drewe a thousand ships to *Troy*, to fetch
her backe with a pestilence. Wise men in *Greece* in the
meane while to swagger so aboute a whore.

Eloquious hoarie beard father *Nestor*, you were one of
them, and you *M. Vlisses* the prudent dwarfe of *Pallas* another, of whome it is *Illiadizd* that your very nose dropt su-
E 4   gar

In olde time they vsed to wring out at any miracle.

gar candie, and that your spittle was honye. *Natalis Comes* if he were aboue ground, would be sworne vpon it. As loude a ringing miracle as the attractiue melting eye of that strũpet can we supply thē with of our dappert *Piemont Huldrick Herring*, which draweth more barkes to Yarmouth bay, then her beautie did to *Troy*. O he is attended vpon most *Babilonically*, and Xerxes so ouercloyd not the *Hellespont* with his foystes, gallies, and brigandines, as he mantleth the narrow seas with his retinue, being not much behinde in the checkroule of his *Ianissaries* and contributories, with Eagle-soaring *Bullingbrooke*, that at his remouing of houshold into banishment (as father *Froysard* threapes vs downe) was accompanied with 40000, men wemen and children weeping, from London to the landes end at Douer. A colony of criticall *Zenos* should they sinnow their sillogisticall clutter-fistes in one bundle to confute and disproue mouing, were they but during the time they might lap vp a messe of buttred fish, in Yarmouth one fishing, such a violent motion of toyling *Mirmidons* they should be spectators of and a confused stirring to and fro, of a *Lapantalike* hoast of vnfatigable flud bickerers

The sea battaile at Lepanta fought in the beginning of her Maiesties raigne.

and foame-curbers, that they woulde not moue or stir one foote till they had disclaimd and abiurd their bedred spittlepositiõs. In verament and sincerity I neuer crouded through this confluent herring faire, but it put me in memory of the great yeare of Iubile in *Edward* the thirds time, in which it is sealed and deliuered vnder the handes of a publique notary, three hundred thousand people romed to Rome for purgatorie pils and paternal veniall benedictions, and the waies beyond sea were so bungd vp with your dayly oratours or *Beads-men* and your crutchet or croutchant friers or crossecreepers and barefoote penitentiaries, that a snaile coulde not wriggle in her hornes betwixt them. Small thinges we may expresse by great, and great by smal, though the greatnesse of the redde herring be not small as small a hoppe on my thumbe as hee seemeth) It is with him as with great personages
sonages

sonages,which from their high estate and not their high sta-
tures.propagate the eleuaute titles of their Gogmagognes,
Cast his state who will and they shall finde it to be very high
coloured(as high coloured as his complexion if I saide there
were not a pimple to be abated)In Yarmouth he hath set vp
his state house,where one quarter of a yeare he keepes open
court for *Iewes* and gentiles.

    To fetch him in,in * *Troian Equipage* some of euery of the
Christ-crosse Alphabet of outlandish *Cosmopoli* furrowe vp
the rugged brine,and sweepe through his tumultuous cous
will or nill hee rather then in tendring their alleagance they
should be benighted with tardity. For our English *Mikro-
kosmos or Phenician Didos* hide of grounde; no shire,county
count palatine,or quarter of it,but rigs out some oken squa-
dron or other to waft him along * *Cleopatraean* * *Olimplickly*,
and not the dimunutiuest nooke or creuise of them but is
parturiët of the like superofficiousnes,*arming forth though
it be but a catch or pinck no capabler then a rundlet or wa-
shing bowle,to impe the wings of his conuoy.*Holy S.Taur-
bard* in what droues the gouty bagd Londoners hurry down
and die the watchet aire of an yron russet hue with the dust
that they raise in hot spurd rowelling it on to performe cô-
plementes vnto him. One becke more to the balies of the
cinque portes,whome I were a ruder *Barbarian* then *Smill*
the Prince of the *Crims & Nagayans* if in this actiô I should
forget (hauing had good cheare at their tables more then
once or twice whiles I loytred in this paragôlesse fish town)
Citty,towne,cuntry, Robin hoode and little Iohn and who
not,are industrious and carefull to squire and safe conduct
him in,but in vshering him in next to the balies of Yarmoth,
they trot before all,and play the prouost marshals helping to
keep good rule the first three weeks of his ingresse, and neuer leaue roaring it out with their brasen horne as long as
they stay,of the freedomes and immunities sousing frô him.
Beeing thus entred or brought in the consistorians or setled
standerds

* The fattall
wodden horse
at Troy fetcht
in with such
pompe.

Cleopatras
glorious say-
ling to meete
Anthony.
*The solemne
bringing of the
champions at
Olimpus.
1.Tugging
forth by the
strength of
their armes.

ſtanders of Yarmouth, commenſe inteſtine warres amongſt
themſelues who ſhould giue him the largeſt hoſpitality, and
gather about him as flocking to hanſell him and ſtrike him
good luck as the Sweetkin Madans did about valiãt *S.Wal-*
ter Manny the martiall tutor vnto the Blacke prince (he that
built Charterhouſe) who being vpon the point of a hazzar-
dous iourney into France, either to win the horſe or loſe the
ſaddle (as it runs in the Prouerb) & taking his leaue at Court
in a ſute of male frõ top to toe, all the ladies clung about him,
and would not let him ſtretch out a ſtep till they had enfet-
tred him with their variable fauours, and embroidred ouer
his armour like a gaudy Summer meade, with three ſcarfes,
bracelets, chains, ouches : in generous reguerdoment wherof he ſacramentally obliged himſelfe, that had the French
king as many giants in his countrey as hee hath peares or
grapes, and they ſtood all enranged on the ſhore to interdiĉt
his diſimbarking, through the thickeſt thornie quickſet of
thẽ he would pierce, or be toſt vp to heauen on their ſpeares,
but in honour of thoſe debonaire Idalian nimphs and their
ſpangled trappings, he would be the firſt man ſhould ſet foot
in his kingdome, or vnſheath ſteele againſt him. As he promiſed ſo was his * manly blades execution, and in emula-
tion of him, whole heards of knights and gentlemen clos'd
vp their right eyes with a piece of ſilke euery one, & vowed
neuer to vncouer them or let thẽ ſee light, til in the aduance-
ment of their miſtreſſe beauties, they had enaĉted with their
brandiſht bilbowblades ſome chiualrous *Bellerophons* trick
at armes, that from Salomons Ilands to S. Magnus corner
might cry clang againe. O it was a braue age then, and ſo it
is euer, where there are offenſiue wars, and not defenſiue, &
men fight for the ſpoile, and not in feare to be ſpoiled, & are
as lions ſeeking out their pray, and not as ſheepe that lie ſtill
whiles they are prayd on. The redde herring is a legate of
peace, and ſo abhorrent from vnnatural bloudſhed, that if in
his quarrell or bandying, who ſhould harbing him, there be
                                                    any

*Manny quaſi
Manly, & from
him I take it
the Mannies of
Kent are de-
ſcended.

any hewing or flafhing, or trials of life & death, there where that hang-man embowelling is, his purfuiuants or balier returne *non eft inuentus*, out of one bailiwick he is fled, neuer to be faftened on there more. The Scotifh Iockies or Red-fhanks (fo furnamed of their immoderate raunching vp the red fhanks or red herrings) vphold & make good the fame. Their clacke or gabbling to this purport : *How in diebus illis, when Robert de Breaux their gudking fent his deare heart to the haly land, for reafon he caud not gang thider himfelfe (or then or thereabout, or whilome before, or whilome after, it matters not) they had the ftaple or fruits of the herring in their road or channell, till a foule ill feud arofe amongft his fectaries and feruitours, and there was mickle tule, and a blacke warld, and a deale of whinyards drawne about him, and many fackleffe wights and praty barnes run through the tender weambs, and fra thence ne farry taile of a herring in thilke found they caud gripe.* This language or parley haue I vfurpt from fome of the deftelt lads in all Edenborough towne, which it will be no impeachment for the wifeft to turne loofe for a trueth, without any diffident wraftling with it. The fumpathy thereunto in our owne frothy ftreames we haue tooke napping, wherfore without any further bolftring or backing, this Scotifh hiftory may beare palme, & if any further bolftring or backing be required, it is euident by the confeffion of the fixe hundred Scotifh witches executed in Scotland at Bartelmewtide was twelue-moneth, that in Yarmouth road they were all together in a plumpe on Chriftmaffe eue was two yere when the great floud was, & there ftird vp fuch *ternados* & *furicanos* of tempefts, in enuy (as I collect) that the ftaple of the herring from them was tranflated to Yarmouth, as will be fpoke of there whiles any winds or ftormes & tempefts chafe & puffe in the lower region. They and all the feafaring townes vnder our temperate zone of peace, may well enuy her profperity, but they cannot march cheeke by iowle with her or coequall her, and ther's no fuch manifeft figne of great profperity as a

generall

generall enuy encompaffing it. Kings,noble-men it cleaues
vnto that walke vpright, and are any thing happy, & euen a-
mongft meane artificers it thrufts in his foot, one of thē en-
uying another if he haue a knack aboue another,or his gains
be greater, and if in his arte they cannot difgrace him, they
will finde a ftarting hole in his life that fhall confound him:

*Iohn Thurkle for example: There is * a mathematicall Smith or artificer in
Yarmouth that hath made a locke and key that weighes but
three farthings, and a cheft with a paire of knit gloues in the
till of it, whofe whole poife is no more but a groat,now I do
not thinke but all the Smiths in London,Norwich or Yorke
(if they heard of him)would enuy him,if they could not cut-

*The Sybarites worke him. *Hydra* herring will haue euery thing * Sybarite
neuer woulde dainty,where he lays knife aboord,or he wil fly them,he wil
make any ban-not looke vpon them. Stately borne,ftately fprung he is,the
quet vnder a beft bloud of the Ptolomies no ftatelier,and with what ftate
twelue-mo-he hath bene vfed from his fwadling clouts,I haue reiterated
neths warn-vnto you, and which is a note aboue *ela,* ftately *Hyperion* or
ing. the lordly fonne,the moft rutilant planet of the feuē,in Lent
when *Heralius* herring enters into his chiefe reign and fcep-
terdome, skippeth and danfeth the goats iumpe on the earth
for ioy of his entrance. Do but marke him on your walles a-
ny morning at that feafon how he fallies & laualtos,and you
wil fay I am no fabler. Of fo eye bewitching a deaurate rud-
die dy is the skincoat of this Lantfgraue, that happy is that
nobleman who for his colours in armory can neereft imitate
his chimicall temper, nay which is more,if a man fhould tell
you that god *Himens* faffron colour'd robe were made of
nothing but red herrings skins, you would hardly beleeue
him : fuch is the obduracy & hardneffe of heart of a number
of infidels in thefe dayes,they wlll teare herrings out of their
skins as faft as one of thefe Exchequer tellers can turne ouer
a heape of money, but his vertues both exterior and interior
they haue no more tafte of, then of a difh of ftockfifh.Some-
where I haue fnatcht vp a ieaft of a king that was defirous to

try

try what kinde of flefh-meat was moft nutritiue profperous
with a mans body,and to that purpofe he commanded foure
hungry fellowes,in foure feparate roomes by themfelues to
bee fhut vp for a yeare and a day, whereof the firft fhoulde
haue his gut bumbafted with biefe and nothing elfe,till hee
cride hold belly holde,and fo the fecond to haue his paunch
cramd with porke, the third with mutton,& the fourth with
veale.At the tweluemonths ende they were brought befoie
him, &he enquired of euery one orderly what he had eat e.
Therewith outftept the ftallfed foreman that had bin at hoft
with the fat oxe, and was growne as fat as an oxe with tiring
on the furloynes,and baft in his face Biefe,Biefe,Biefe,Next
the Norfolke hog or the fwine-wurrier, who had got him a
fagging paire of cheeks like a fows paps that giues fuck,with
the plentyfull maft fet before him, came lazily wadling in,
and puft out Porke, Porke,Porke.Then the fly fheepe-biter
iffued into the midft,and fummer fetted & fliptflapt it twenty times aboue ground as light as a feather and cride mitton,
mitton, mitton, laft the Effex calfe or lagman, who had loft
the calues of his legs with gnawing on the horflegs,fhudring
and quaking limpte after, with a vifage as pale as a peece of
white leather,and a ftaffe in his hande and a kirchiefe on his
head,and very lamentably vociferated veale,veale,veale. A
witty toy of his noble grace it was, and different from the
recipes and prefcriptions of our moderne phifitions, that to
any ficke languifhers if they be able to waggle their chaps,
propound veale for one of the higheft nourifhers.

But had his principalitie gone thorough with fifh as well
as flefh, and put a man to liuery with the red herring but as
long,he would haue come in *Hurrey*,*Hurrey*,*Hurrey*, as if he
were harrying and chafing his enemies,& *Beuis* of *Hampton*
after he had bene out of his diet , fhould not haue bene able
to haue ftood before him. A chollericke parcell of food it is ,
that who fo ties himfelfe to racke and manger to for fiue
fummers, and fiue winters,he fhall beget a child that will be
a fouldiour and a commaunder before hee hath caft his firft
teeth,

As much to fay
as Vrrey,Vr-
rey, Vrrey one
of the princi-
pall places
where the her-
ring is caught.

teeth, & an *Alexander*, a *Iulius Cæſar*, a *Scanderbega Barba-
roſſa* he will proue ere he aſpire to thirtie,

But to thinke on a red Herring, ſuch a hot ſtirring meate
it is, is enough to make the craueneſt daſtard proclaime fire
and ſword againſt Spaine. The moſt intenerate Virgine wax
phiſnomy, that taints his throate with the leaſt ribbe of it, it
will embrawne and Iron cruſt his fleſh, and harden his ſoft
bleeding vaines as ſtiffe and robuſtious, as branches of Cor-
rall. The art of kindling of fires that is practiſed in the ſmoking or parching of him, is old dog againſt the plague. Too
foule-mouthed I am to be collow or be collier, him with ſuch
chimnie ſweeping attributes of ſmoking and parching. Wil
you haue the ſecrete of it, this well meaning *Pater patriæ*, &
prouiditore and ſupporter of Yarmouth (which is the locke
and key of Norfolke) looking pale and ſea-ſicke at his firſt
landing, thoſe that be his ſtewards or neceſſarieſt men about
him, whirle him in a thought out of the raw colde ayre, to
ſome ſtew or hot houſe, where immuring himſelfe for three
or foure dayes, when he vn-houſeth him, or hath caſt off his
ſhel, he is as freckled about the gils, & lookes as red as a Fox,
dumme & is more ſurly to be ſpoken with then euer he was
before, and like *Lais* of Corinth, will ſmile vpon no man except he may haue his owne asking. There are that number
of Herrings vented out of Yarmouth euery yeare (though
the Grammarians make no plurall number of *Halec*) as not
onely they are more by two thouſand Laſt then our owne
land can ſpend, but they fil all other lands, to whome at their
owne priſes they ſell them, and happie is he that can firſt lay
hold of them. And how can it bee otherwiſe, for if Corniſh
Pilchards otherwiſe called *Fumados*, taken on the ſhore of
Cornewall, from Iuly to Nouember, bee ſo ſaleable as they
are in Fraunce, Spaine and Italy, (which are but countefets
to the red Herring as Copper to Golde, or Ockamie to ſiluer, much more, there elbows itch for ioy, when they meete
with the true Golde, the true red Herring it ſelfe. No true
flying fiſh but he, or if there be, that fiſh neuer flies but when
his

his wings are wet, and the red Herring flyes beſt when his
wings are dry, throughout Belgia, high Germanie, Fraunce,
Spaine and Italy hee flyes, and vp into Greece, and Africa
South , and Southweſt , Eſtritch-like walkes his ſtations,
and the Sepulcher, Palmers or Pilgrims , becauſe hee is ſo
portable fill their Scrips with them , yea no diſpraiſe to the
bloud of the *Ottamans*, the *Nabuchedoneſor* of Conſtantino-
ple, and Giantly *Antæus* that neuer yawneth nor neezeth
but he affrighteth the whole earth, gormandizing muncheth
him vp for imperiall dainties, and will not ſpare his Idol *Ma-
homet* a bit with him,no not though it would fetch him from
heauen fortie yeares before his time, whence with his Doue
that he taught to pecke Barley out of his eare, and brought
his Diſciples into a fooles paradiſe,that it was the holy ghoſt
in her ſimilitude,he is expected euery minute to diſcend,but
I am affraid, as he was troubled with the falling ſickneſſe,in
his life time , in ſelfe manner it tooke him in his mounting
vp to heauen, & ſo *ab inferno nulla redemptio*,he is falne back-
ward into hell,and they are neuer more like to heare of him.
Whiles I am ſhuffling and cutting with theſe long coated
Turkes , would any antiquarie would explicate vnto mee
this remblere or quidditie , whether thoſe *Turbanto* grout-
heads, that hang all men by the throates on Iron hookes, e-
uen as our Toers hang all there Herrings by the throates
on wodden ſpits, firſt learnd it of our Herring men, or our
herringmen of them. Why the Alcheronſhip of that Belza-
bub of *Saracens*, *Rhinoceros Zelim* aforeſaid,ſhould ſo much
delight in this ſhinie animall I cannot geſſe, except hee had
a deſire to imitate *Midas* in eating of gold, or *Dioniſius* in
ſtripping of *Iupiter* out of his golden Coate ; and to ſhoote
my fooles bolt amongſt you, that fable of *Midas* eating gold
had no other ſhadow or incluſiue pith in it, but he was of a
queaſie ſtomacke, and nothing hee coulde fancie, but this
newe found guilded fiſh, which *Bacchus* at his requeſt gaue
him, (though it were not knowne here two thouſand yeare

Turbanto, the
great Iawne
roule Turkes
were aboute
their heads.

after

after, for it was the delicates of the gods, & no mortall foode til of late yeares) *Midas* vnexperienſt of the nature of it, (for he was a foole that had aſſes eares) ſnapt it vp at one blow, & becauſe in the boyling or ſeathing of it in his maw, he felt it commotion a little and vpbraide him, he thought he had eaten golde in deede, and thereupon directed his Orizons to *Bacchus* afreſh, to helpe it out of his crop againe , and haue mercy vpon him and recouer him, hee propenſiue inclining to *Midas* deuotion in euery thing, in lieu of the friendly hoſpitalities, drunken *Silenus* his companion found at his hands when he ſtrayed from him , bad him but goe waſh himſelfe in the riuer *Pactolus*, that is, goe waſh it downe ſoundly with flowing cups of Wine and he ſhould be as well as euer hee was. By the turning of the riuer *Pactolus* into golde, after he had ren'ſt and clarified himſelfe in it (which is the cloſe of the fiction) is ſignified that in regard of that bleſſed operation of the iuice of the grape in him, from that day forth in nothing but golden cups he would drinke or quaffe it, whereas in wodden Mazers, and *Agathocles* earthen ſtuffe, they trillild it off before, and that was the firſt time that any golden cups wer vſed.

Follow this tract in expounding the tale of *Dioniſius* and *Iupiter*, and you cannot goe amiſſe. No ſuch *Iupiter*, no ſuch golden coated image was there : but it was a plaine golden coated red herring without welt or garde, whome for the ſtrangenes of it (they hauing neuer beheld a beaſt of that hue before) in their temples inſhrined for a God, and in ſomuch as *Iupiter* had ſhewed thē ſuch ſlippery pranckes more then once or twiſe, in ſhifting himſelfe into ſundry ſhapes, and rayning himſelfe downe in golde into a womans lappe, they thought this too might be a tricke of youth in him , to alter himſelfe into the forme of this golden *Scali-ger*, or red herring. And therefore as to *Iupiter* they fell downe on their marybones, & lift vp their hay-cromes vnto him. Now king *Dioniſius* being a good wiſe-fellow, for he was afterwards a ſchoolemaſter, & had plaid the coatchman to *Plato* & ſpit in

Ariſtip-

Ariſtippus the Philoſophers face many a time and oft, no ſooner entred their tẽple, & ſaw him ſit vnder his Canopie ſo budgely with a whole Goldſmiths ſtall of iewelles and rich offerings at his feete, but to him he ſtept, and pluckt him from his ſtate with a wennion, then drawing out his knife moſt iracundiouſly, at one whiske lopt off his head, and ſtript him out of his golden deiny or mandillion, and flead him, and thruſt him downe his pudding houſe at a gobbe : yet long it proſpered not with him, (ſo reuengefull a iuſt Iupiter is the red Herring) for as he tare him from his throne, and vncaſed him of his habilimenrs, ſo in ſmal deuolution of yeres, from his throne was he chaced, and cleane ſtript out of his royalty,& glad to go play the Schoolemaiſter at Corinth, and take a rodde in his hand for his ſcepter, and horne-booke Pigmeis for his ſubieĉts, *id eſt*, (as I intimated ſome dozen lines before) of a tyrant to become a frowning pedant or ſchoolemaiſter.

Many of you haue read theſe ſtories, and coulde neuer picke out any ſuch Engliſh, no more woulde you of the Iſmael Perſians Haly, or *Mortus Alli*, they worſhip, whoſe true etimologie is, *mortuum halec*, a dead red herring, and no other, though by corruption of ſpeech, they falſe dialeĉt and miſſe-ſound it. Let any Perſian oppugne this, and in ſpite of his hairie tuft or loue-locke he leaues on the top of his crowne, to be pulld vp, or pullied vp to heauen by, Ile ſet my foot to his,& fight it out with him,that their fopperly god is not ſo good as a red Herring. To recount *ab ouo*, or from the church-booke of his birth, howe the Herring firſt came to be a fiſh, and then how he came to be king of fiſhes,and gradionately,how from white to red he changed, would require as maſsie a toombe as Hollinſhead, but in halfe a penniworth of paper I

G   wil

will epitomize them. Let me fee, hath any bodie in Yarmouth heard of Leander and Hero, of whome diuine *Musæus* fung, and a diuiner Mufe than him, *Kit Marlow*?

Twoo faithfull louers they were, as euerie apprentife in Paules churchyard will tell you for your loue, and fel you for your mony : the one dwelt at Abidos in Afia, which was Leander , the other which was Hero, his Miftris or Delia, at Seftos in Europe, and fhe was a pretty pinckany and Venus prieft ; and but an arme of the fea diuided them : it diuided them and it diuided them not , for ouer that arme of the fea could be made a long arme. In their parents the moft diuifion refted, and their townes that like Yarmouth and Leyftoffe were ftil at wrig wrag, & fuckt frō their mothers teates ferpentine hatred one againft each other. Which droue Leander when he durft not deale aboue boord, or be feene aboorde any fhip, to faile to his Lady deare, to play the didopper and ducking water fpaniel to fwim to her, nor that in the day, but by owlelight.

What will not blinde night doe for blinde Cupid? and what will not blinde Cupid doe in the night which is his blindmans holiday? By the fea fide on the other fide ftoode Heroes tower, fuch an other tower as one of our Irifh caftles , that is not fo wide as a belfree, and a Cobler cannot iert out his elbowes in ; a cage or pigeonhoufe, romthfome enough to comprehend her and the toothleffe trotte her nurfe , who was her onely chatmate and chambermaide; confultiuely by her parents being fo encloiftred frō refort, that fhe might liue chafte veftall Prieft to Venus the queene of vnchaftitie. Shee would none of that fhe thanked them, for fhee was better prouided , and that which they thought ferued their turn beft of fequeftring her

から from

from company, ferued her turne beft to embrace the
company fhe defired. Fate is a fpaniel that you cannot beate from you; the more you thinke to croffe it,
the more you bleffe it, and further it.

Neither her father nor mother vowed chaftitie
when fhe was begote, therefore fhe thought they be-
gat her not to liue chafte,& either fhe muft proue hir
felfe a baftard,or fhew her felfe like them.Of Leander
you may write vpon, and it is written vpon, fhe likte
well, and for all he was a naked man, and cleane dif-
poyled to the skinne, when hee fprawled through the
brackifh fuddes to fcale her tower, all the ftrength of
it could not hold him out. O ware a naked man, Ci-
thereaes Nunnes haue no power to refifte him : and
fome fuch qualitie is afcribed to the lion. Were hee
neuer fo naked when he came to her, bicaufe he fhuld
not skare her, fhe found a meanes to couer him in her
bed,& for he might not take cold after his fwimming,
fhe lay clofe by him, to keepe him warme. This fcuf-
fling or bopeepe in the darke they had a while without weame or bracke, and the olde nurfe (as there bee
three things feldome in their right kinde till they bee
old,a bawd,a witch,and a midwife)executed the huck
ftring office of her yeres very charily & circumfpect-
ly til their fliding ftarres reuolted from them:and then
for feauen dayes togither, the winde and the Hellef-
pont contended which fhuld howle lowder,the waues
dafhed vp to the cloudes, and the clouds on the other
fide fpit and driueld vpon them as faft.

Hero wept as trickling as the heauens, to thinke
that heauen fhould fo diuorce them. Leander ftor-
med worfe than the ftormes, that by them hee fhould
be fo reftrained from his Cinthya. At Seftos was his
foule, and hee coulde not abide to tarry in Abidos.
Rayne, fnowe, haile, or blowe it howe it could,

into

into the pitchie Helefpont he leapt when the moone
and all her torch-bearers were afraide to peepe out
their heads; but he was peppered for it, hee hadde as
good haue tooke meate, drinke, and leifure, for the
churlifh frampold waues gaue him his belly full of
fifh-broath, ere out of their laundry or wafhe-houfe
they woulde graunt him his coquet or *tranfire*, and
not onely that, but they feaide him his *quietus eft*,for
curuetting any more to the mayden tower,and tofled
his dead carcaffe, well bathed or parboyled, to the
fandy threfhold of his leman or orenge, for a difiune
or morning breakfaft. All that liue long night could
fhe not fleepe, fhe was fo troubled with the rheume,
which was a figne fhe fhould heare of fome drowning:
Yet towards cocke-crowing fhe caught alittle flum-
ber, and then fhee dreamed that Leander and fhee
were playing at checkeftone with pearles in the bottome of the fea.

You may fee dreames are not fo vaine as they are
preached of, though not in vaine,Preachers inueigh
againft them, and bende themfelues out of the peo-
ples mindes, to exhale their foolifh fuperftition.The
rheume is the ftudents difeafe, and who ftudy moft,
dreame moft. The labouring mens hands,glowe and
blifter after their dayes worke : the glowing and bli-
ftring of our braines after our day labouring cogita-
tions are dreames, and thofe dreames are reaking va-
pours of no impreffion, if our mateleffe cowches bee
not halfe empty. Hero hoped, and therefore fhee
dreamed (as all hope is but a dreame) her hope was
where her heart was, and her heart winding and
turning with the winde, that might winde her heart
of golde to her, or elfe turne him from her. Hope
and feare both combatted in her, and both thefe are
wakefull, which made her at breake of day (what an
olde

old crone is the day, that is so long a breaking) to vn-
loope her luket or casement, to looke whence the
blasts came, or what gate or pace the sea kept, when
foorthwith her eyes bred her eye-sore, the first white
whereon their transpiercing arrowes stuck, being the
breathlesse corps of *Leander* : with the sodaine con-
templation of this piteous spectacle of her loue , sod-
den to haddocks meate, her sorrowe could not choose
but be indefinite, if her delight in him were but indif-
ferent; and there is no woman but delights in sorrow,
or she would not vse it so lightly for euery thing.

Downe shee ranne in her loose night-gowne, and
her haire about her eares (euen as *Semiramis* ranne out
with her lie-pot in her hand, and her blacke dangling
tresses about her shoulders with her iuory combe en-
snarled in them, when she heard that *Babilon* was taken) and thought to haue kist his dead corse aliue a-
gaine, but as on his blew iellied sturgeon lips, she was
about to clappe one of those warme plaisters, boy-
strous woolpacks of ridged tides came rowling in, and
raught him from her, (with a minde belike to carrie
him backe to *Abidos*.) At that she became a franticke
Bacchanal outright, & made no more bones but sprang
after him, and so resignd vp her Priesthood, and left
worke for *Musæus* and *Kit Marlowe*. The gods, and
gods and goddesses all on a rowe bread and crow, from
Ops to *Pomona*, the first applewife, were so dumpt
with this miserable wracke, that they beganne to ab-
horre al moysture for the seas sake : and *Iupiter* could
not endure *Ganimed* his cup-bearer to come in his pre-
sence, both for the dislike he bore to *Neptunes* baneful
licour, as also that hee was so like to *Leander*. The
sunne was so in his mumps vppon it, that it was
almost noone before hee could goe to cart that day,
and then with so ill a will hee went , that hee had

thought

thought to haue topled his burning catre or Hurrie
currie into the fea(as *Phaeton* did)to fcorch it and dry
it vppe, and at night when hee was begrimed with
duft and fweate of his iourney, he would not defcend
as hee was woont, to wafh him in the Ocean, but vnder a tree layde him downe to reft in his cloathes all
night, and fo did the fcouling Moone vnder another
faft by him, which of that are behighted the trees of
the Sunne and Moone, and are the fame that Syr
Iohn Mandeuile tels vs hee fpoke with,and that fpoke
to *Alexander. Venus,*for *Hero* was her prieft, and *Iuno
Lucina* the midwifes goddefse,for fhe was now quick-
ned, and caft away by the cruelty of *Æolus* , tooke
bread and falt and eate it,that they would bee fmartlie
reuenged on that truculent windy iailour, and they
forgot it not,for *Venus* made his fonne and his daugh-
ter to committe inceft together . *Lucina,* that there
might bee fome lafting charaſters of his fhame,helpt
to bring her to bedde of a goodly boy , and *Æolus*
boulting out al this , heapt murder vppon murder.

The dint of deftiny could not be repeald in the re-
uiuing of *Hero* & *Leander,* but their heauenly hoods
in theyr fynode thus decreede, that for they were either of them feaborderers and drowned in the fea,ftil
to the fea they muft belong, and bee diuided in habitation after death , as they were in their life
time. *Leander,* for that in a cold darke teftie night he
had his pafport to *Charon,* they terminated to the vnquiet cold coaft of Ifeland , where halfe the yeare is
nothing but murke night, and to that filh tranflated
him,which of vs is termed Ling. *Hero,* for that fhe was
pagled and timpanized, and fuftained two loffes vnder one,they footebald their heades togither, & pro-
tefted to make the ftem of her loynes of all fifhes the
flanting Fabian or Palmerin of England, which is
Cad-

Cadwallader Herring, and as their meetings were but
feldome, and not fo oft as welcome, fo but feldome
fhould they meete in the heele of the weeke at the
beft mens tables, vppon Fridayes and Satterdayes, the
holy time of Lent exempted, and then they might be
at meate and meale for feuen weekes togither.

The nurfe or mother Mampudding that was a cow-
ring on the backe fide whiles thefe things were a tra-
gedizing, led by the fcritch or outcry to the profpect
of this forrowfull heigho, as foone as through the
raueld button holes of her bleare eyes, fhe had fuckt
in & receiued fuch a reuelatiõ of Doomefday, & that
fhe faw her miftris mounted a cockhorfe, & hoyfted
away to hell or to heauen on the backs of thofe rough
headed ruffians, down fhe funk to the earth, as dead as
a doore naile, and neuer mumpt cruft after. Whereof
their fupernalities (hauing a drop or two of pitty left
of the huge hogfhead of teares they fpent for *Hero* &
Leander) feemed to be fomething forie, though they
could not weepe for it, and becaufe they would bee
fure to haue a medicine that fhould make them weep
at all times, to that kinde of graine they turned her,
which wee call muftard-feede, as well for fhee was a
fhrewifh fnappifh bawd, that wold bite off a mãs nofe
with an anfwere, and had rumatique fore eyes that ran
alwaies, as that fhe might accompany *Hero* & *Leander*
after death, as in hir life time: & hẽce it is that muftard
bites a mã fo by the nofe, & makes him weep & water
his plants when he tafteth it: & that *Hero* & *Leander*,
the red Herring and Ling, neuer come to the boord
without muftard, their waiting maid: & if you marke
it, muftard looks of the tanned wainfcot hue, of fuch
a withered wrinklefaced beldam as fhe was, that was
altred thereinto. Louing Hero, how euer altered, had
a fmack of loue ftil, & therfore to the coaft of louing-
                                                    land

land (to Yarmouth neere adioyning, & within her
liberties of Kirtley roade) ſhe accuſtomed to come in
pilgrimage euery yeare, but contentions ariſing there,
and ſhee remembring the euent of the contentions
betwixt *Seſtos* and *Abidos*, that wrought both *Le-
anders* death and hers, ſhunneth it oft late, and retireth
more northwards, ſo ſhe ſhunneth vnquiet Humber,
becauſe *Elſtred* was drownd there, and the Scots Seas,
as before, & euery other ſea where any bloud hath bin
ſpilt, for her owne ſeas ſake, that ſpilt her ſweete
ſweete hearts bloud and hers.

Whippet, turne to a new leſſon, and ſtrike wee vp
Iohn for the King, or tell howe the Herring ſcram-
bled vp to be King of all fiſhes. So it fel vpon a time
and tide, though not vppon a holiday, a faulco-
ner bringing ouer certaine hawkes out of *Ireland*,
and airing them aboue hatches on ſhip-boord, and giuing them ſtones to caſt & ſcoure, one of them broke
looſe from his fiſt ere he was aware, which beeing in
her Kingdome when ſhee was got vppon her wings,
and finding her ſelfe emptie gorged after her caſting,
vp to heauen ſhe towred to ſeeke pray, but there being no game to pleaſe her, downe ſhe fluttered to the
ſea againe, and a ſpeckled fiſh playing aboue the water, at it ſhe ſtrooke, miſtaking it for a partrich. A
ſharke or Tuberon that lay gaping for the flying fiſh
hard by, what did me he, but ſeeing the marke fall ſo
iuſt in his mouth, chopt aloft, and ſnapt her vp belles
and all, at a mouthfull. The newes of this murderous
act, carried by the Kings fiſher to the eares of the
land foules, there was nothing but arme, arme, arme,
to ſea, to ſea, ſwallow & titmouſe, to take chaſticemēt
of that treſpaſſe of bloud & death committed againſt
a peere of their bloud royal. Preparation was made,
the muſter taken, the leaders allotted, and had their
bils

bils to take vp pay;an old goſhawke for general was appointed, for Marſhall of the field a Spaihawke, whom for no former deſert they putte in office, but becauſe it was one of their linage had ſuſtained that wrong, and they thought they would be more implacable in condoling and commiſerating. The Peacocks with their ſpotted coates and affrighting voyces for heralds they prickt and enliſted , and the cockadoodling cocks for their trumpeters, (looke vpon any cocke,and looke vpon any trumpeter, and ſee if hee looke not as red as a cocke after his trumpeting,and a cocke as red as he after his crowing.) The kiſtrilles or windfuckers that filling themſelues with winde,fly againſt the winde euermore, for their fulſailed ſtanderdbearers, the Cranes for pikemen, and the woodcocks for demilances,and ſo of the reſt euery one according to that place by nature hee was moſt apt for. Away to the landes ende they trigge all the ſkie-bred chirpers of them, when they came there,*Æquora nos terrent & ponti triſtis imago,* They had wings of good wil to fly with, but no webbes on their feete to ſwimme with, for except the waterfoules had mercie vpon them, and ſtood their faithſull confederates and backe-friends, on their backes to tranſport them, they might returne home like good fooles, and gather ſtrawes to build their neſts, or fal to theyr old trade of picking wormes. In ſum, to the water foules vnanimately they recourſe,and beſought Ducke, and Drake, Swanne and Gooſe Halcions & Seapies,Cormorants & Sea-guls of their oary aſſiſtance,& aydeful furtherance in this action.

They were not obdurate to be intreated, though they had little cauſe to reuenge the hawkes quarrell from them, hauing receiued ſo many high diſpleaſures,and ſlaughters, and rapines of their race,

H   yet

yet in a generall profecution priuate feuds they
trode vnderfoote, and fubmitted their endeuors to be
at theyr limitation in euery thing.

The puffin that is halfe fifh, halfe flefh (a Iohn in-
different, and an *Ambodexter* betwixt either) bewray-
ed this confpiracie to *Protæus* heards, or the fraternity
of fifhes, which the greater giants of Rufsia & Ifland,
as the whale, the fea horfe, the Norfe, the wafferman,
the Dolphin the Grampoys fleered and geered at as
a ridiculous danger, but the leffer pigmeis & fpawne
of them, thought it meete to prouide for themfelues
betime, and elect a king amongft them that might
deraine them to battaile, and vnder whofe colours
they might march againft thefe birdes of a feather,
that had fo colleagued themfelues togither to deftroy
them.

Who this king fhould bee, befhackled theyr
wits, and layd them a dry ground euery one. No ra-
uening fifh they would putte in armes, for feare
after he had euerted their foes, and flefht himfelfe in
bloud, for interchange of diet, hee woulde rauen vp
them.

Some politique delegatory Scipio, or witty pated
Petito, like the heire of *Laertes per apherefin, Vlyffes,*
(well knowne vnto them by his prolixious feawan-
dering, and daunching on their topleffe tottering
hilles) they would fingle forth, if it might bee, whom
they might depofe when they lift, if he fhould begin
to tyranize, and fuch a one as of himfelfe were able
to make a found partie if all fayled, and bid bafe to
the enemie with his owne kindred and followers.

None woonne the day in this but the Herring,
whom al their clamorous fuffrages faluted with *Viue
le roy,* God faue the King, God faue King, faue only
the Piayfe and the Butte, that made wry mouthes at
                                                    him

him, and for their mocking haue wry mouthes euer
since,and the Herring euer since weares a coronet on
his head, in token that hee is as he is .Which had the
worst end of the staffe in that sea iourney or canua-
zado, or whether some fowler with his nets(as this
host of fethermungers were getting vp to ride double)inuolued or intangled them, or the water foules
playde them false (as there is no more loue betwixt
them, then betwixt saylers and land souldiours) and
threw them off their backs, and lette them drowne
when they were launched into the deepe, I leaue to
some *Alfonsus*) *Poggius* or *Æsope* to vnwrap,for my
penne is tired in it:but this is notorious, the Herring
from that time to this,hath gone with an army, and
neuer stirres abroade without it , and when he stirs
abroad with it, he sendes out his scowts or sentinels
before him,that oftentimes are intercepted, and by
theyr parti-coloured liueries descried,whom the ma-
riners after they haue tooke , vse in this sort : eight
or nine times they swinge them about the maine
mast, and bid them bring them so many last of Herrings as they haue swinged them times, and that shall
be theyr ransome, and so throw them into the sea; a-
gaine. King by your leaue, for in your kingshippe I
must leaue you, and repeate how from white to redde
you camelionized.

It is to bee read, or to bee heard of, howe in the
Punieship or nonage of Cerdicke sandes, when the
best houses and walles there were of mudde or can-
uaze,or Poldauies entiltments, a Fisherman of Yarmouth hauing drawne so many herrings hee wist not
what to do withall,hung the residue that he could not
sel nor spéd, in the sooty roofe of his shad a drying:or
say thus, his shad was a acbbinet in *decimo sexto*, builded on foure crutches,and hee had no roome in it,but
in that garret or *Excelsis* to lodge them,where if they

were drie, let them bee drie, for in the sea they had
drunke too much, and now hee would force them doe
penance for it.

The weather was colde, and good fires hee kept,
(as fishermen, what hardnesse soeuer they endure at sea, they will make all smoake, but they
will make amendes for it when they come to
land) and what with his fiering and smoking, or smo-
kie firing in that his narrow lobby, his herrings which
were as white as whales bone when hee hung them
vp, nowe lookt as red as a lobster. It was foure or fiue
dayes before either hee or his wife espied it, & when
they espied it, they fell downe on their knees & bles-
sed themselus, & cride, a miracle, a miracle, & with the
proclaiming it among their neighbours they could
not be content, but to the court the fisherman would,
and present it to the King, then lying at *Borrough* Castle two mile off.

Of this *Borrough* Castle, because it is so auncy-
ent, and there hath beene a Citie there, I will enter
into some more speciall mention. The floud Waueny running through many Townes of hie Suffolke
vp to *Bungey*, and from thence incroching neerer and
neerer to the sea, with his twining & winding it cuts
out an Iland of some amplitude, named Louingland.
The head Towne in that Iland is *Leyftofe*, in which
bee it knowne to all men I was borne, though my
father sprang from the *Nashes* of Herefordshire.

The next Towne from *Leyftofe* towardes Yarmouth is *Corton*, and next *Gorlston*. More inward-
ly on the left hande, where Waueny and the riuer
Ierus mixe their waters, *Cnoberi vrbs*, the Cittie of
Cnober, at this day termed *Burgh* or *Borough* Castle, had his being.

This cittie and castle saith *Bede* and Maister *Camden*, or rather M. *Camden* out of *Bede*, by the woodes
about

about it , and the driuing of the fea vppe to it , was moſt pleaſant. In it one Furfæus a Scot builded a monaſtery, at whoſe perſwaſion Sigebert king of the eaſt Angles, gaue ouer his kingdome and led a mona. ſticall life there, but forth of that monaſtery hee was haled againſt his will, to incourage his ſubieꝭts in their battaile againſt the Mercians, where he periſhed with them.

Nothing of that Caſtle ſaue tartered ragged walles nowe remaines, framed foure ſquare, and ouergrowne with briars and buſhes, in the ſtubbing vp of which, erſt whiles they digge vppe Romane coynes, and booies and anchors. Well, thither our Fiſherman ſet the beſt legge before , and vnfardled to the King, his whole ſachel of wonders. The King was as ſuperſtitious in worſhipping thoſe miraculous herrings as the fiſherman, licenced him to carry thē vp & downe the realme for ſtrange monſters, giuing to Cerdek ſands (the birth place of ſuch monſtroſities) many priuileges, and in that the quantitie of them that were caught ſo encreaſed, he aſſigned a broken ſluce in the Iland of Louingland , called Herring Fleete , where they ſhoulde disburden and diſcharge their boates of them, and render him cuſtome. Our Herring ſmoker hauing worn his monſters ſtale throughout England, ſpirted ouer ſeas to Rome with a Pedlers packe of thē in the Papall chaire of *Vigilius* , he that firſt inſtituted Saints eeues or Vigils to be faſted. By that time hee came thither, he had but three of his Herrings left, for by the way he fell into the theeuiſh hands of malcontents, and of launceknights, of whom he was not only robbed of all his mony , but was faine to redeeme his life beſides with the better parte of his ambry of burniſht fiſhes

Theſe herrings three he rubbed and curried ouer

till his armes aked againe, to make them glowe and
glare like a Turkie brooch, or a London Vintners
ſigne, thicke iagged, and round fringed, with theam-
ing Arſadine, and folding them in a diaper napkin
as lilly white as a Ladies marrying ſmocke, to the market ſteade of Rome he was ſo bold as to prefer them,
and there on a hie ſtoole, vnbraced and vnlaced them,
to any chapmans eie that woulde buye them . The
Popes caterer caſting a licorous glaunce that way, aſ-
ked what it was he had to ſell: the king of fiſhes hee
anſwered : the king of fiſhes replied hee, what is the
price of him? A hundred duckats he tolde him : a hundred duckats queth the Popes caterer, that is a kingly
price indeede, it is for no priuate man to deale with
him : then hee is for mee ſayde the Fiſherman, and ſo
vnſheathed his cuttle-bong, and from the nape of
the necke to the taile diſmembred him, and pauncht
him vp at a mouthfull. Home went his Beatitudes caterer with a flea in his eare, and diſcourſed to his Ho-
lineſſe what had happened. Is it the king of fiſhes?
the Pope frowningly ſhooke him vp like a catte in a
blanket, and is any man to haue him but I that am
king of kings, and lord of lords? Go giue him his price
I commaund thee, and lette mee taſte of him inconti-
nently. Backe returned the Caterer like a dogge that
had loſt his taile, and powred downe the herringmer-
chant his hundred ducats for one of thoſe two of the
king of fiſhes vnſolde, which then he would not take,
but ſtoode vppon twoo hundred. Thereuppon they
broke off, the one vrging that he had offered it him ſo
before, and the other, that hee might haue tooke him
at his proffer, which ſince he refuſed, and now halperd
with him : as he eate vp the firſt, ſo would he eate vpp
the ſecond, and let Pope or patriarch of Conſtantino-
ple fetch it out of his belly if they could : Hee was as
good

good as his word, and had no sooner spoke the worde,
but he did as he spoke. With a heauy heart to the pallace the yeoman of the mouth departed, and rehear-
sed this second il succeffe, wherwith Peters succeffour
was so in his mulliegrums that he had thought to haue
buffeted him, & cursed him with bell book & candle,
but he ruled his reaso, & bade him, thogh it cost a million, to let him haue that third that rested behind, and
hie him expeditely thither, lest some other snatched it
vp, and as fast from thence againe, for hee swore by
his triple crowne, no crumme of refection woulde he
gnaw vpon, till he had sweetened his lippes with it.

So said, so done, thither he flew as swift as Mercury,
and threw him his two hundred ducats, as hee before
demaunded. It would not fadge, for then the market
was raised to three C. and the Caterer grumbling
thereat, the fisher swayne was forward to fettle him to
his tooles, and tire vpon it, as on the other two, had not
he held his hands, and desired hym to keep the peace
for no mony should part them : with that speech hee
was quallified, and pursed the three hundred ducats,
and deliuered him the king of fishes, teaching hym
howto geremumble it, sawce it, and dresse it, and so
sent him away a glad man. All the Popes cookes in
their white sleeues and linnen aprons met him middle
way, to entertaine and receyue the king of fishes, and
together by the eares they went, who shoulde first
handle him or touch him: but the clarke of the kichin
appeased that strife, and would admit none but him
selfe to haue the scorching and carbonadoing of it,
and he kissed his hand thrice, and made as many *Hum-*
blessos ere hee woulde finger it : and such obeysances
performed, he drest it as he was enioyned, kneeling
on his knes, and mumbling twenty aue Maryes to
hymselfe in the sacrifizing of it on the coales, that his

dili-

diligent ſeruice in the broyling and combuſtion of i'ꝭ both to his kingſhip and to his fatherhood might not ſeeme vnmeritorious. The fire had not perſt it, but it being a ſweaty loggerhead greaſie ſowter, endūgeond in his pocket a tweluemonth, ſtunk ſo ouer the popes pallace, that not a ſcullion but cryed foh, and thoſe which at the firſt flocked the faſteſt about it, now fled the moſt from it, and ſought more to rid theyr hands of it, than before they ſought to bleſſe theyr handes with it. Wyth much ſtopping of theyr noſes, between two diſhes they ſtued it, and ſerued it vp. It was not come wythin three chambers of the Pope, but he ſmelt it, and vpon the ſmelling of it enquiring what it ſhould be that ſent forth ſuch a puiſſant perfume, the ſtanders by declared that is was the king of fiſhes: I conceyted no leſſe ſayde the Pope, for leſſe than a king he could not be that had ſo ſtrong a ſent, and if his breath be ſo ſtrong, what is he hymſelf? like a great king, like a ſtrong king I will vſe hym, let hym be caried backe I ſay, and my Cardinalls ſhall fetch hym in with dirge and proceſſions vnder my canopy.

Though they were double and double weary of hym, yet his Edict being a lawe, to the kitchin they returned him, whither by and by the whole Colledge of ſcarlet Cardinalles, wyth theyr croſiers, theyr cenſors, their hoſts, their *Agnus deies* and crucifixes, flocked togither in heapes as it had beene to the conclaue or a generall counſaile, and the ſenior Cardinall that ſtood next in election to bee Pope, heaued him vp from the Dreſſer with a dirge of *De profundis natus eſt ſex, rex* he ſhould haue ſayd, and ſo haue made true latine, but the ſpirable odor & peſtilent ſteame aſcending from it, put him out of his bias of congruity, & as true as the trueſt latin of *Priſcian* would haue queazened him, like the dampe that tooke both *Bell*

and

and Baram away, and many a woorthy man that day,
it hee had not beene protected vnder the Popes canopy, and the other Cardinalles with theyr holi-wa-
ter sprinkles, quencht his foggy fume and euapora-
ting. About and about the inward and base court
they circumducted him, with *Kirielyson* and *Halleluiah*,
and the chaunters in their golden copes and white
surplesses, chaunted it out aboue *gloria patri,* in pray-
sing of him, the Organs playde, the Ordonance at
the Castle of Saint *Angelos* went off, and all wind in-
struments blew as loude as the winde in winter, in
his passado to the Popes ordinary or dining chamber, where hauing sette him downe, vppon their fa-
ces they fell flatte, and lickt euery one his ell of dust,
in douking on all foure vnto him.

The busie epitasis of the commedy was, when the
dishes were vncouered, and the swarthrutter sowre
tooke ayre, for then hee made such an ayre, as *Alcides*
himselfe that clensed the stables of *Agæus* nor any
hostler was able to endure.

This is once, the Pope it popt vnder boord, and
out of his pallace worse it scared him then *Neptunes
Phocases,* that scard the horses of *Hippolitus,* or the
harpies *Iupiters* dogges sent to vexe *Phineus;* the Cardinalles were at their *ora pro nobis,* and held this suffo-
cation a meete sufferance for so contemning the king
of fishes and his subiects, and fleshly surfetting in
their carniualles. Negromantick sorcery, negroman-
ticke sorcerie, some euill spirit of an heretique it is,
which thus molesteth his Apostoliqueship. The fri-
ars and munkes caterwawled from the abbots and
priors to the nouices, wherfore *tanquam in circo,* wee
will trownse him in a circle, and make him tell what
Lanterneman, or groome of Hecates close stoole hee
is, that thus nefariously and proditoriously prophani-

I   ning

ning &penetrates our holy fathers nosttils, what
needes there any more ambages, the ringoll or rin-
ged circle was compast and chalkt out, and the king
of fishes by the name of the king of fishes, coniured
to appeare in the center of it, but *furdo cantant abfur-
di, fiue furdum incantant fratres fordidi*, hee was a king
abfolute, and would not be at euery mans cal, & if frier *Pendela* and his fellowes had any thing to fay to
him, in his admiral court of the fea, let them feek him,
and neither in Hull, Hell, nor Halifax.

They feeing that by theyr charmes and fpels they
could fpell nothing of him, fell to a more charitable
fuppofe, that it might bee the diftreffed foule of
fome king that was drownd, who being long in Purgatorie, and not releeued by the praiers of the church,
had leaue in that difguifed forme, to haue egreffe
and regreffe to Rome, to craue theyr beneuolence of
dirges, trentals, and fo foorth, to helpe him on-
ward on his iourney to *Limbo patrum* or *Elifium*, and
becaufe they would not eafily beleeue what tortures
in purgatory hee had fuftained, vnleffe they were
eye-witneffes of them, hee thought to reprefent to
all theyr fences the image and *Idea* of his combuftion
and broyling there, and the horrible ftinch of his fins
accompanying both vnder his frying and broyling
on the coles in the Popes kitchin, & the intollerable
fmel or ftink he fent forth vnder either. *Una voce* in
this fplene to Pope *Vigilius* they ran, and craued that
this king of fifhes might firft haue Chriftian buriall,
next, that hee might haue maffes fung for him, and
laft, that for a faint hee would canonize him. Al thefe
hee graunted, to bee ridde of his filthy redolence, and
his chiefe casket wherein he put all his iewelles, hee
made the coffin of his enclofure, and for his enfain-
ting, looke the Almanack in the beginning of Aprill,

and

and fee if you can finde out fuch a faint as faint *Gil-darde*, which in honour of this guilded fifh the Pope fo enfainted: nor there hee refted and ftopt, but in the mitigation of the very embers wheron he was findged, that after he was taken of them, fumed moft fulfomly of his fatty droppings,)hee ordained ember weekes in their memory, to be fafted euerlaftingly.

I had well nie forgot a fpeciall poynt of my Romifh hiftory, & that is how Madam *Celina Cornificia*, one of the curiofeft curtizans of Rome, when the fame of the king of fifhes was canon-rored in her eates, fhee fent all hir iewells to the iewifh lumbarde to pawne, to buy and encaptiue him to her trenchour, but her puruey our came a day after the faire, & as he came, fo hee farde, for not a fcrap of him but the cobs of the two Herrings the Fifherman had eaten remained of him, and thofe Cobbes, rather than hee woulde go home wyth a fleeuelefle anfwer, he bought at the rate of fourefcore ducats (they were rich cobbes you muft rate them) and of them all cobbing countrey chuffes which make their bellies and their bagges theyr Gods are called riche Cobbes. Euery manne will not clappe hands to this itale, the Norwichers inprimis, who fay, the firft guilding of Herrings was deducted from them: and after this guife they tune the accent of theyr fpeech; how that when Caftor was Norwich (a Towne twoo mile beyond this Norwich, that is termed to this day Norwich Caftor, and hauing monuments of a caftle in it enuironing fifty acres of ground, and ringbolts in the walles whereto fhips were faftned) our Norwich now vpon her leggs was a poore fifher towne, and the fea fpawled and fpringed vp to her common ftayres in Confur ftreete.

All this may paffe in the Queenes peace, and no man fay bo to it: but bawwaw quoth Bagfhaw to that
I 2   which

which drawlacheth behinde, of the firſt taking of herrings there, and currying and guylding them amongſt
thē, wherof if they could whiſper to vs any ſimple like-
lihood, or rawbond carcaſſe of reaſon, more than their
imaginary dreame of Guilding croſſe in theyr pariſh
of S. Sauiours (now ſtumpt vp by the rootes) ſo named, as they would haue it, of the ſmoaky guilding of
herrings there firſt inuented, I could wel haue allowed
of, but they muſt bring better cardes ere they winne
it from Yarmouth.

　　As good a toy to mocke an ape was it of hym that
ſhewed a country fellow the red ſea, where all the red
Herrings were made (as ſome places in the ſea where
the ſunne is moſt tranſpercing, and beates wyth his
rayes feruenteſt, will looke as red as blood:) and the
ieaſt of a Scholler in Cambridge, that ſtanding ang-
ling on the towne bridge there, as the country people
on the market day paſſed by, ſecretly bayted his hook
wyth a red Herring wyth a bell about the necke, and
ſo conueying it into the water that no man perceiued
it, all on the ſodayn, when he had a competent throng
gathered about hym, vp he twicht it agayne, and layd
it openly before them, whereat the gaping rurall
fooles, driuen into no leſſe admiration than the common people about Londō ſome few yeares ſince were
at the bubbling of Moore-ditch, ſware by their chri-
ſtendomes that as many dayes and yeeres as they had
liued, they neuer ſawe ſuch a myracle of a red herring
taken in the freſh-water before. That greedy ſeagull
ignorance is apt to deuoure any thing. For a new Meſ-
ſias they are ready to expect of the bedlam hatmakers
wife by London bridge, he that proclaymes hymſelfe
Elias, and ſayeth he is inſpired wyth mutton and por-
redge, and with them it is currant, that Don Sebaſtian
king of Portugall (ſlayne twenty yeares ſince wyth
　　　　　　　　　　　　　　　　　　　　Stukely

Stukeley at the battell of Alcazar) is rayfed from the
dead like Lazarus, and aliue to be feene at Venice. Let
them looke to themfelues as they will, for I am theirs
to gull them better than euer I haue done, and this I
am fure I haue deftributed gudgeon dole amongft
them, as Gods plenty as any ftripling of my flender portion of witte farre or neere. They needes
will haue it fo, much good do it them, I can not doe
wythall : For if but careleſly betwixt ſleeping and
waking I write I knowe not what againſt plebeian
Publicans and finners (no better than the fworne bro-
thers of candleſticke turners and tinkers) and leaue
fome termes in fufpence that my poft-hafte want of
argent will not giue mee elbowe roome enough to
explane or examine as I would, out fteps me an infant
fquib of the Innes of Court, that hath not halfe grea-
fed his dining cappe, or fcarce warmed his Lawyers
cufhion, and he to approue hymfelfe an extrauagant
ftatefman catcheth hold of a ruſh, aud abfolutely con-
cludeth, it is meant of the Emperour of Rufcia, and
that it will vtterly marre the traffike into that country
if all the Pamphlets bee not called in and fuppreſſed,
wherein that libelling word is mentioned. An other,
if but a head or a tayle of any beaft, he boaſts of in his
creſt or his fcutcheon, be reckoned vp by chaunce in
a volume where a man hath iuft occaſion to reckon vp
all beafts in armory, he ftrait engageth hymfelfe by
the honor of his houfe, and his neuer reculed fword
to threfh downe the hayry roofe of that brayne that
fo feditiouſly mutined againſt hym with the mortife-
rous baftinado, or caft fuche an vncurable Italian
trench in his face, as not the bafeft creeper vpon pat-
tens by the high way fide, but fhall abhor him worfe
than the carrion of a dead corfe, or a man hanged vp
in gibbets.

I will deale more boldly, & yet it shall be securelie, and in the way of honestie, to a number of Gods fooles, that for their wealth might be deep wise men, and so foorth (as now a daies in the opinion of the best lawyers of England there is no wisedome without wealth, alleadge what you can to the contrarie of all the beggarly sages of greece) these I say out of some discourses of mine, which were a mingle mangle cum purre, and I knew not what to make of my selfe, haue fisht out such a deepe politique state meaning as if I had al the secrets of court or common-wealth at my fingers endes. Talke I of a beare, O it is such a man that emblazons him in his armes, or of a woolfe, a fox, or a camelion, any lording whom they do not affect, it is meant by. The great potentate stirred vppe with those peruerse applications, not looking into the text it selfe, but the ridiculous comment, or if hee lookes into it, followes no other more charitable comment then that, straite thunders out his displeasure, & showres downe the whole tempest of his indignation vpon me, and to amend the matter, and fully absolue himselfe of this rash error of misconstruing, he commits it ouer to be prosecuted by a worse misconstruer then himselfe, *vidilicet*, his learned counsaile (God forgiue me if I slander them with that title of learned, for generally they are not) and they being compounded of nothing but vociferation and clamour, rage & fly out they care not howe against a mans life, his person, his parentage, twoo houres before they come to the poynt, little remembring their owne priuy scapes with their landresses, or their night walkes to Pancredge, togither with the hobnaylde houses of their carterly ancestrie from whence they are sprung, that haue coold plow-iades buttocks time out of minde, with the breath of their whistling, and with retailing their

theyr dung to manure landes, and felling ſtrawe and
chaffe,ſcracht vp the pence to make them gentlemen,
But Lord howe miſerably do theſe Ethnicks when
they once march to the purpoſe,ſet words on the ten-
ters,neuer reading to a period (which you ſhal ſcarſe
find in thirtie ſheetes of a lawyers declaration) wher-
by they might comprehende the intire ſence of the
writer togither, but diſioynt and teare euery ſillable
betwixt their teeth ſeuerally, and if by no meanes
they can make it odious,they wil be ſure to bring it in
diſgrace by ilfauoured mouthing and miſſounding it.
Theſe bee they that vſe mens writings like bruite
heaſts, to make them draw which way they liſt, as a
principall agent in church controuerſies of this
our time complaineth. I haue red a tale of a poore
man and an aduocate, which poore man complained
to the King of wrong that the aduocate hadde doone
him,in taking away his cow. The king made him no
anſwere but this, that hee woulde ſende for the aduocate,and heare what hee could ſay. Nay quoth the
poore man, if you bee at that paſſe that you wil pawſe
to heare what he wil ſay,I haue vtterly loſt my cowe,
for hee hath woords inough to make fooles of tenne
thouſand. So hee that ſhal haue his lines bandied
by our vſuall plodders in Fitzherbart, lette him
not care whether they bee right or wrong : for
they will writhe and turne them as they liſt,and make
the author beleeue he meant that which hee neuer did
meane : and for a knitting vp concluſion, his credite is
vnrepriueably loſt, that on bare ſuſpitiõ in ſuch caſes,
ſhal but haue his name controuerted amongeſt thē, &
if I ſhould fall into their handes, I would be preſſed to
death for obſtinate ſilence, and neuer ſeeke to cleere
my ſelfe, for it is in vaine, ſince both they will confound a mans memory wyth their tedious babbling,
and

and in the firſt three wordes of his Apology with im-
pudent exclamations interrupt him , whenas their
mercenary tongues(lie they neuer ſo lowdly) without
checke or controule muſt haue their free paſſage for
fiue houres together.

I ſpeake of the worſer ſort, not of the beſt,whom
I holde in high admiration, as well for theyr ſingular
gifts of art and nature, as theyr vntaynted conſciences
wyth corruption : and from ſome of them I auowe I
haue heard as excellent things flowe, as euer I obſer-
ued in Tully or Demoſthenes. Thoſe that were preſent at the arraignmēt of Lopus, (to inſiſt in no other
particular) hereof I am ſure will beare me record. La-
tineleſſe dolts ſaturnine heauy headed blunderers,my
inuectiue hath relation, to ſuch as count al Artes pup-
pet-playes , and pretty rattles to pleaſe children, in
compariſon of their confuſed barbarous lawe, which
if it were ſet downe in any chriſtian language, but the
Getan tongue it would neuer grieue a man to ſtudie
it.

Neyther *Ouid* nor *Arioſto* coulde by any perſwaſi-
ons of their parents be induced to ſtudy the Ciuil law
for the harſhneſſe of it,how much more,(had they bin
aliue at this day,and borne in our nation) weuld they
haue conſented to ſtudy this vnciuill Norman hot-
porch, this ſow of lead, that hath neuer a ring at the
end to lift it vp by,is without head or foote,the defor-
medeſt monſter that may bee. I ſtand lawing heere
what with theſe lawyers,and ſelfe-conceited miſinter-
preters ſo long, that my redde herring which was hot
broyling on the coles, is waxt ſtarke cold for want
of blowing.Haue with them for a riddle or two,onely
to ſet their wittes a nibbling, and their iobbernowles
a working,and ſo good night to their ſegniories, but
with this indentment and caution, that though there
be

be neither rime nor reason in it, (as by my good will
there shal not) they according to their accustomed
gentle fauors, whether I wil or no, shall supply it with
either, and runne ouer al the peeres of the land in pee-
uish moralizing and anatomizing it.

There was a Herring, or there was not, for it was
but a cropshin, one of the refuse sort of herrings, and
this herring or this cropshin was sensed and thurified
in the smoake, and had got him a suit of durance, that it
would last longer then one of *Erra Paters* Alma-
nacks, or a cunstables browne bill, onely his head was
in his tayle, and that made his breath so strong, that
no man could abide him. Well, he was a *Triton* of his
time, and a sweete singing calander to the state, yet
not beloued of the snoury *Pleyades* or the *Colossus* of
the sunne, howeuer hee thought himselfe another
tumidus Antimachus, as compleate an *Adelautado* as hee
that is knowne by wearing a cloake of tuftaffatie
eighteene yeare, and to Lady *Turbut* there is no de-
murre but he would needs goe a wooing, and offered
her for a dowre whole hecatombs and a twoo-hand-
sword, shee starde vpon him with *Megaras* eyes, like
Iris the messenger of *Iuno*, and bad him go eate a fookes
head and garlick, for she would none of him, thereuppon particularly strictly and vsually he replied, that
though thunder nere lights on *Phœbus* tree, and *Am-
phion* that worthy musition, was husband to *Niobe*, and
there was no such acceptable incense to the heauens
as the bloud of a traitour, reuenged hee would bee
by one *Chimera* of imagination or other, and ham-
per and embrake her in those mortal straights for hir
disdain, that in spite of diuine simnietry & miniature,
into her buskie groue shee should let him enter, and
bid adew sweete Lord, or the crampe of death should
wrest her heart strings.

This fpeech was no fpireable odor to the *Achelous* of her audience, wherefore fhe charged him by the extreame lineaments of the Erimanthian beare, and by the priuy fiftula of the *Pierides,* to committe no more fuch excruciating fillables to the yeelding ayre, for fhe would fooner make her a French.hood of a cowfharde and a gowne of fpiders webbes, with the fleeues drawn out with cabbages,then be fo contaminated any more with his abortiue loathely motiues: With this in an olympick rage, he calles for a cleane fhirt,and puttes on fiue paire of buskins, and feeketh out eloquent *Zenophon,* out of whofe mouth the Mufes fpake , to declaime in open Courte againft her.

The action is entred, the complaint of her wintered browes prefented, of a violent rape of his heart fhee is indited and conuinced. The circumftaunce that followes you may imagine or fuppofe : or without fuppofing or imagining, I will tell you, the nutte was crackt, the ftrife difcuft, and the center of her heart layd open,and to this wild of forrowes and excruciament fhe was confined, either to bee helde a flat thornebacke, or fharpe pricking dog-fifh to the weale publique, or feale her felfe clofe to his fealeskind riueld lippes, and fuffer her felfe as a fpirit to be coniured into the hellifh circle of his embraces.

It would not be good cropfhin, Madam *Turbut* could not away with fuch a drie withered carkaffe to lie by her,*currat rex,viuat lex,*come what would, fhee would none of him, wherfore as a poyfoner of mankind with her beautie,fhe was adiudged to be boyled to death in hot fcalding water, and to haue her pofterity throughly fawft and fowft and pickled in barrelles of brinifh teares, fo ruthfull and dolorous, that

the

the inhabitants on *Bofphoros* fhould bee laxatiue in deploring it. O for a Legion of mice-eyed decipherers and calculaters vppon characters, now to augurate what I meane by this; the diuell, if it ftood vppon his faluation cannot do it, much leffe petty diuels, and cruell Rhadamants vppon earth, (elfe where in France and Italy *fubintelligitur*, and not in our afpicious Iland climate) men that haue no meanes to purchafe credit with theyr Prince, but by putting him ftill in feare, and beating into his opinion, that they are the onely preferuers of his life, in fitting vp night and day in fifting out treafons, whe they are the moft traytours themfelues, to his life, health, and quiet, in continual commacerating him with dread and terror, when but to gette a penfion, or bring him in theyr debt next to God, for vpholding his vital breath, it is neither fo, nor fo, but fome foole, fome drunken man, fome madde man in an intoxicate humour hath vttered hee knewe not what, and they beeing ftarued for intelligence, or want of employment, take hold of it with tooth and nayle, and in fpite of all the wayters, will violently breake into the kings chamber, and awake him at midnight to reueale it.

Say that a more piercing Linceus fight fhould diue into the intrailes of this infinuating parafites knauery; to the ftrapado and the ftretching torture, hee will referre it for triall, and there eyther teare him limbe from limbe, but hee will extract fome capitall confefsion from him, that fhal concerne the Princes life, and his crowne and dignity, and bring himfelfe in fuch neceffary requeft about his prince, as hee may holde him for his right hand, and the onely ftaffe of his royalty, and thinke hee were vndoone if hee were without him, when the poore fellow fo tyrannonfly handled, would rather in that extremitie of conuulfion, confeffe hee crucified Iefus Chrift, then abide it any longer. I am not againft it,(For God forbid I fhould) that it behooues all loyall true fubiects to bee vigilant and iealous for their princes fafetie, and certaine too iealous and vigilant of it they cannot bee, if they bee good princes that raigne ouer them, nor vfe too many meanes of difquifition by tortures, or otherwife to difcouer treafons pretended againft them, but vppon the leaft wagging of a ftraw to put them in feare where no feare is, and make a hurliburlie in the realme vpon had I wift, not fo much for any zeale or loue to their princes, or tender care of theyr preferuation, as to picke thankes, and curry a little fauour, that thereby they may lay the foundation to build a fute on, or croffe fome great enemie they haue, I will maintaine it is moft lewd and deteftable. I accufe none, but fuch there haue beene belonging to Princes in former ages, if there bee not at this houre.

Stay, let me looke about, where am I in my text, or out of it? not out for a groate: out for an angell, nay I'le lay no wagers, for nowe I perponder more fadlie vppon it, I thinke I am out indeede. Beare with it, it was but a pretty parenthefis of Princes and theyr parafites, which fhall doo you no harme, for I will cloy you with Herring before wee part.

Will you haue the other riddle of the cropfhin to make vppe the payre that I promifed you, you fhall you fhall (not haue it I meane)but beare with mee, for I cannot fpare it, and I perfwade my felfe you wil be weil contented to fpare it, except it were better then the former, and yet I pray you what fault can you finde with the former, hath it any more fence in it then it fhould haue? is it not right of the merry coblers cutte in that witty Play of, *the Cafe is altered.*

I

I will fpeake a proude word (though it may bee counted arrogancy in me to prayfe mine owne ftuffe) if it bee not more abfurde then *Philips his Venus,* *the white Tragedie, or the greene Knight,* or I can tell what Englifh to make of it in part or in whole; I wifh in the fouleft weather that is, to goe in cutte fpanifh lether fhooes, or filke ftockings, or to ftand barehead to a nobleman, and not gette of him the price of a periwig to couer my bare crown, no not fo much as a pipe of Tabacco to rayfe my fpirites, and warme my braine.

My readers peraduenture may fee more into it then I can, for in comparifon of them, in whatfoeuer I fet forth, I am *Bernardus non vidit omnia,* as blinde as blinde Bayard, and haue the eyes of a beetle, nothing from them is obfcure, they being quicker fighted then the funne, to fpie in his beames the moates that are not, and able to transforme the lighteft murmuring gnat to an Elephant. Carpe or defcant they as theyr fpleene mooues them, my fpleene mooues me not to file my handes with them, but to fall a crafh more to the redde herring.

Howe many bee there in the worlde that childifhly depraue Alchumy, and cannot fpell the firft letter of it; in the black booke of which ignorant band of fcorners, it may be I am fcorde vp with the higheft, if I be, I muft intreate them to wipe me out, for the red herring hath lately beene my ghoftly father to conuert me to their fayth: the *probatum eft* of whofe transfiguration *ex Luna in Solem,* from his duskie tinne hew into a perfit golden blandifhment, onely by the foggy fmoake of the groffeft kind of fire that is, illumines my fpeculatiue foule, what muche more, not fophifticate or fuperficiall effects, but abfolute effentiall alterations of mettalles there may bee

K 3 made

made by an artificiall repurified flame, and diuerse other helpes of nature added besides.

Cornelius Agrippa maketh mention of some Philosophers that held the skinne of the sheepe that bare the golden fleece, to be nothing but a booke of Alcumy written vpon it, so if wee should examine matters to the proofe, wee shoulde finde the redde Herrings skinne to be little lesse : the accidens of Alcumy I will sweare it is, be it but for that experiment of his smoaking alone, and which is a secret that all Tapsters will curse mee for blabbing, in his skinne there is plaine witchcraft, for doe but rubbe a kanne or quarte pot round about the mouth wyth it, let the cunningest lickespiggot swelt his heart out, the beere shal neuer foame or froath in the cupp, whereby to deceyue men of their measure, but be as setled as if it stoode al night.

Next, to draw on hounds to a sent, to a redde herring skinne there is nothing comparable. The round or cobbe of it dride and beaten to powlder is *ipse ille* agaynst the stone : and of the whole body of it selfe, the finest Ladies beyond seas frame their kickshawes.

The rebel Iacke Cade was the first that deuised to put redde herrings in cades, and from hym they haue their name. Nowe as wee call it the swinging of herrings when hee cade them, so in a halter was hee swung, and trussed vppe as hard and round as any cade of herring he trussed vppe in his tyme, and perhappes of his being so swung and trussed vp, hauyng first found out the tricke to cade herring, they woulde so much honour him in his death, as not onely to call it swinging, but cading of herring also. If the text will beare this, we wil force it to beare more, but it shall be but the weight of a strawe, or the weight of *Iacke Straw* more, who with the same *Graca fide* I marted

vnto

vnto you the former, was the firſt that putte the redde
herring in ſtraw ouer head and eares like beggars, &
the Fiſhermen vpon that Iacke ſtrawd him euer after:
& ſome, for he was ſo begarly a knaue that chalenged
to be a gentleman, and had no witte nor wealth but
what hee got by the warme wrapping vp of herring,
raiſed this Prouerbe of him, *Gentleman Iacke Herring
that puttes his breeches on his head for want of wearing.* O-
ther diſgraceful prouerbes of the herring there be, as,
*Nere a barrell better herring : Neither fleſh nor fiſh, nor
good red herring,* which thoſe that haue bitten with ill
bargaines of either ſort, haue dribd forth in reuenge,
and yet not haue them from Yarmouth, many coaſt
towns beſides it, enterpriſing to curry ſalt and pickle
vp herrings, but marre them, becauſe they want the
right feate how to ſalt and ſeaſon them. So I coulde
plucke a crowe wyth Poet *Martiall* for calling it *pu-
tre halec,* the ſcauld rotten herring, but he meant that
of the fat really Scottiſh herrings, which will endure
no ſalt, and in one moneth (beſtow what coſt on them
you wil) waxe ramiſh if they be kept, whereas our
embarreld white herrings, flouriſhing with the ſtate-
ly brand of Yarmouth vpon them, *ſcilicet* the three
halfe Lions and the three halfe fiſhes with the crowne
ouer the head, laſt in long voyages, better than the
redde herring, and not onely are famous at *Roan, Pa-
ris, Diepe, Cane* (whereof the firſt, which is *Roan,* ſer-
ueth all the high countries of Fraunce with it, and
Diepe which is the laſt ſaue one, victualles all *Pi-
cardy* with it) but heere at home is made account of
like a Marqueſſe, and receiued at court right ſolemn-
ly, I care not much if I rehearſe to you the maner, and
that is thus.

Euery yeare about Lent tide, the ſherifes of Norwich bake certayne herring pies (foure and twenty as

I take it) and ſend them as a homage to the Lorde of
Caſter hard by there, for lands that they hold of him,
who preſently vpō the like tenure, in bouncing ham-
pers couered ouer with his cloth of armes, ſees them
conueyed to the court in the beſt equipage: at court
when they are arriued, his man rudely enters not at
firſt, but knocketh very ciuilly, and then officers come
and fetch him in with torch light, where hauing diſ-
fraughted and vnloaded his luggage, to ſupper he ſets
him downe like a Lord, with his waxe lights before
him, and hath his meſſe of meate allowed him with
the largeſt, & his horſes (*quatenus* horſes) are prouen-
dred as epicurely: after this, ſome foure marke fee
towardes his charges is tendred him, and hee iogges
home againe merrily.

A white pickled herring? why it is meate for a
Prince, *Hauuce Vandernecke* of Roterdame (as a dutch
Poſt informed me) in bare pickled herring layd out
twenty thouſand pound the laſt fiſhing: hee had loſt
his drinking belike, and thought to ſtore himſelfe of
medicines enow to recouer it.

Noble Cæſarean Charlemaine herring, *Plinie* and
Geſner were too blame they ſluberd thee ouer ſo neg-
ligently. I do not ſee why any man ſhould enuy thee,
ſince thou art none of theſe *lurcones* or *epulones*, glutōs
or fleſhpots of Egypt (as one that writes of the chri-
ſtians captiuity vnder the Turke enſtileth vs Engliſh
mē) nor liueſt thou by the vnlyuing or euiſcerating of
others, as moſt fiſhes do, or by any extraordinary filth
whatſoeuer, but as the Cameleon liueth by the ayre,
and the Salamander by the fire, ſo onely by the water
arte thou nouriſhed, and nought elſe, and muſt ſwim
as wel dead as aliue.

Be of good cheere my weary Readers, for I haue e-
ſpied land, as *Diogenes* ſaid to his weary Schollers whē
he

the red Herring.   73

he had read to awafte leafe. Fifhermen I hope wil not
finde fault with me for fifhing before the nette, or ma-
king all fifh that comes to the net in this hiftory, fince
as the Athenians bragged they were the firft that inuented wraftling: and one *Ericthonius* amongft them
that he was the firft that ioyned horfes in collar cou-
ples for drawing, fo I am the firft that euer fette quill
to paper in prayfe of any fifh or fifherman.

   Not one of the Poets aforetime could giue you or
the fea a good word : *Ouid* fayth, *Nimium ne credite
ponto*, the fea is a flippery companion take heed how
you truft him : And further, *Periurij pœnas repetit ille
locus*, it is a place like Hel, good for nothing but to pu-
nifh periurers ; with innumerable inuectiues more
againft it throughout in euery booke.

   Plautus in his *Rudens* bringeth in fifhermen cow-
thring and quaking dung wet after a ftorme, and com-
plaining their miferable cafe in this forme, *Captamus
cibum è mari, fi euentus non venit, neque quicquam cap-
tum eft piscium, falfi lautiq́, domum redimus clanculnm,
dormimus incœnatum* : All the meate that we eate we
catch out of the fea, and if there wee miffe, wel wafhed
and falted, wee fneake home to bed fupperleffe : and
vpon the taile of it hee brings in a parafite that flowt-
eth and bourdeth them thus : *Heus vos familica gens ho-
minum vt viuitis vt peritis?* hough you hungerftarued
gubbins or offalles of men, how thriue you, howe pe-
rifh you, and they cringing in their neckes, like rattes,
fmothered in the holde, poorely replicated, *Viuimus
fame, speq́, fitiq́,* with hunger, and hope, and thirft wee
content our felues. If you would not mifconceit that
I ftudiously intended your defamation, you fhoulde
haue thicke hailefhot of thefe.

   Not the lowfie riddle wherewith fifhermen con-
ftrayned (fome fay) *Homer*, fome fay another Philo-

            L   fopher

fopher to drowne hymfelfe, becaufe he could net ex-
pound it,but fhould be dreffed and fet before you *fu-*
pernagulum, with eight fcore more galliarde croffe-
poynts, and kickfhiwinfhes of giddy eare-wig brains,
were it not I thought you too fretfull and chollericke
with feeding altogether on falt meates, to haue the fe-
crets of your trade in publique difplayed. Will this
appeafe you, that you are the predeceffors of the A-
poftles, who were poorer Fifhermen than you , that
for your feeing wonders in the deepe, you may be the
fonnes and heires of the Prophet Ionas, that you are
all Caualiers and Gentlemen fince the king of fifhes
vouchfafed you for his fubiects , that for your felling
fmoake you may be courtiers, for your keeping of fa-
fting dayes Friar Obferuants, and laftly, that looke
in what Towne there is the figne of the three mari-
ners, the huffe-cappeft drink in that houfe you fhal
be fure of alwayes.

No more can I do for you than I haue done, were
you my god-children euery one : God make you his
children and keepe you from the Dunkerks, and then
I doubt not but when you are driuen into harbour by
foule weather , the kannes fhall walke to the health
of *Nafhes* Lenten-ftuffe , and the praife of the redde
Herring, and euen thofe that attend vppon the pitch-
kettle, will bee druncke to my good fortunes, and re-
commendums. One boone you muft not refufe mee
in, (if you be *boni focij* and fweete Oliuers) that you
let not your ruftie fwordes fleepe in their fcabberds,
but lafh them out in my quarrell as hotely, as if you
were to cut cables, or hew the main maft ouer boord,
when you heare mee mangled and torne in mennes
mouthes about this playing with a fhettlecocke, or
tofsing empty bladders in the ayre.

Alas poore hungerftarued Mufe, wee fhall haue
some

some spawne of a goose-quill or ouer worne pander quirking and girding, was it so hard driuen that it had nothing to feede vpon but a redde herring? another drudge of the pudding house (all whose lawfull meanes to liue by throughout the whole yeare will scarce purchase him a redde herring) sayes I might as well haue writte of a dogges turde (in his teeth surreuerence.) But let none of these scumme of the subvrbs, be too vineger tarte with mee; for if they bee, Ile take mine oath vppon a redde herring and eate it, to prooue that their fathers, their grandfathers, and their great grandfathers, or any other of their kinne, were scullions dishwash, & durty draffe and swil set against a redde herring. The puissant red herring, the golden *Hesperides* red herring, the *Meonian* red herring, the red herring of red Herrings Hal, euery pregnant peculiar of whose resplendent lande and honour, to delineate and adumbrate to the ample life, were a woorke that would drinke drie fourescore and eighteene Castalian fountaines of eloquence, consume another *Athens* of facunditie, and abate the haughtiest poeticall fury twixt this and the burning Zone, and the tropike of Cancer. My conceit is cast into a sweating sickenesse, with ascending these few steps of his renowne : into what a hote broyling saint Laurence feuer would it relapse then, should I spend the whole bagge of my winde in climbing vp to the lofty mountaine creast of his trophees. But no more winde will I spend on it but this, Saint Denis for Fraunce, Saint Iames for Spaine, Saint Patrike for Ireland, Saint George for England, and the red Herring for Yarmouth.

(*.*)

FINIS.